A HISTORY OF
UPMINSTER
AND CRANHAM

MANOR

OF

UPMINSTER HALL

NOTICE!

No persons are entitled to depasture Live Stock upon the Common or Waste Lands of the Manor, excepting those tenants holding land within the Manor to which rights of pasture are annexed. The Horses, Cattle, and other Stock belonging to strangers, and found trespassing or straying upon the aforesaid Common or Waste Lands will be impounded, and penalties levied on the owners.

Gipsies, Hawkers, and others encamping on the said Lands, and Damaging the Turf by lighting Fires or otherwise, will be Prosecuted.

BY ORDER,

W. C. CLIFTON,

STEWARD.

ROMFORD, JANUARY, 1885.

WILSON & WHITWORTH, STEAM PRINTERS, ROMFORD, STRATFORD, AND BRENTWOOD.

A HISTORY of UPMINSTER and CRANHAM

John Drury

IAN HENRY PUBLICATIONS

ISBN 0 86025 405 4

ACKNOWLEDGEMENTS

Bruce Anderson for reprographic services
Len Eaton for artwork
Len Boutell and Miss G Hestle for the loan of photograph

Printed for
Ian Henry Publications, Ltd.
20 Park Drive, Romford, Essex RM1 4LH
by
Minerva Press, 9 Tallon Road, Hutton, Brentwood, Essex

PREFACE

The sources of local history are many. Physical remains can be quite interesting in themselves, but they can only tell so much without further research. Oral information from residents, and especially senior citizens whose own memory can often recall people and places going back fifty years or so, is invariably rewarding. The older generation can often recall what their parents told them, which can mean recollections back into the Victorian era. Besides memories old residents can sometimes produce old photographs which, in addition to the main subject of the photograph, may show in the background buildings long since demolished or scenes of countryside or village now greatly changed.

By far the most comprehensive source of information is that of documentary evidence either in manuscript or book form. The study of archives has, since 1945, been eased for students of local history as most County Halls have established an Archive Department. Additionally, the central library of a district contains comprehensive local history material. The Public Record Office and the British Library, with national records of judicial, legal and financial proceedings going back to the 11th century, may not at first appeal to the local historian as a principal source of material, but as the student delves deeper into the history of his locale he or she may find a need to explore these avenues and the student should, at least, find out from these sources what their archives contain in order that no research stone is left unturned.

The Record Office - in our case the County Record Office at Chelmsford - is probably the best source of information on local history. Records at Chelmsford are generally divided into county (judicial and administrative archives of the Courts of Quarter and Petty

Sessions), borough and parish records. In bygone days, before local government was as sophisticated as it is now, the various Sessions at County level dealt with administrative problems, such as bridges, gaols, highways, the poor, markets and hospitals. The Parish, as a unit of local government, is fast dying, but the records maintained in this category are by far the most important. Many parish records have been lost forever, but County Archivists have been gathering all old parish records into the Record Offices for proper cataloguing and repair, if necessary. Parish Council records give much information on the poor of the parish and their welfare, roads and police, etc. The church records are ecclesiastical archives and records of births, marriages and death prior to 1837 could be found in the parish church, although many of these documents are now deposited at Chelmsford. Since 1837 registration has been a civil matter and these records were previously kept at Somerset House and, now, at St Catherine's House, Aldwych. The Vestry Minutes, forerunners of the Parish Council, although administered by the Church, contained items of civil administration and interesting information about residents can be revealed through this source.

Private records are more and more finding their way into Record Offices. The break-up of the large estates for building development in the earlier part of this century has meant that family papers often going back hundreds of years have passed to County Archivists for preservation. Lords of the Manor for centuries held their own courts and these Court Rolls show much about the personalities of yesteryear. These family archives often disclose title deeds, maps of estate, plans of houses and general papers, like letters and receipts, all of which build into a picture of yesterday's village.

Further sources are wills - here we are introduced to the Probate Registers - and Census Returns, Registers of Electors, Rate Books and many other returns that have been made over the years that show who lived where, when and what they owned. This is by no means an exhaustive list of sources of reference, but it does give some idea to an historian where the main repositories are and what subjects can be researched.

In compiling this book I have brought together

much of what has been written before. The work done by the Upminster Branch of the Workers' Educational Association in compiling their 14 volumes of *The Story of Upminster* provided the foundation for my own effort and their research has saved me much time in searching for original records. Dr H E Priestley was closely associated with the research during the production of the volumes between 1957 and 1962 and, during this time, wrote his own fictional book, *John Stranger*, based on Upminster at the time of the Napoleonic Wars in 1803.

Many others, not least Ted Ballard, have contributed to placing Upminster's history in print and most of these are listed in the Sources of Reference. I apologise if I have left someone out.

This little book covers about a thousand years of Upminster and Cranham's history and, consequently, cannot be a comprehensive record of everything that has happened in that time. Ted Ballard, for example, had concentrated on 19th and 20th century Upminster and I cannot compete with the photographs included in his two publications: consequently I have produced only a few to give the flavour of that period. The 14 volumes of *The Story of Upminster* are packed with more information than I have covered, although the pattern is similar to my own effort and, for further research, these out-of-print books are to be found in Havering reference libraries.

The Victoria County History series has published many volumes and, although these include a good history of both Upminster and Cranham, the price of this particular volume is rather prohibitive.

I have thus tried to produce a brief history of the villages going back to the Domesday Book of the 11th century to include what I feel will be of interest to local residents, old and new.

John Drury
Upminster, 1986.

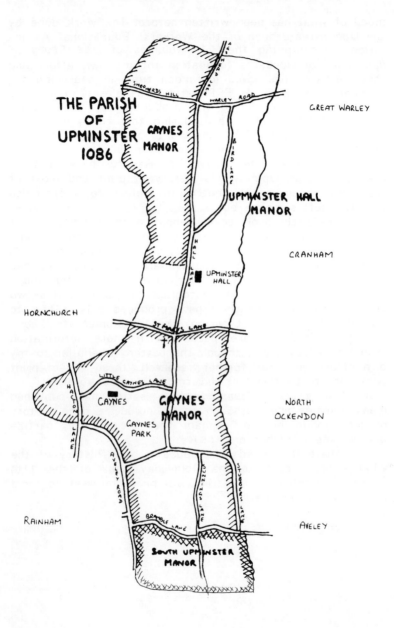

THE PARISH
OF
UPMINSTER
1086

GAYNES MANOR

GREAT WARLEY

SHEPHERDS HILL
ASH HEATH LANE
WARLEY ROAD

BIRD LANE

UPMINSTER HALL MANOR

HALL LANE

UPMINSTER HALL

CRANHAM

HORNCHURCH

ST MARY'S LANE

LITTLE GAYNES LANE

HACTON LANE

GAYNES

GAYNES MANOR

GAYNES PARK

NORTH OCKENDON

AVELEY ROAD

CORBETS LANE
STUBBERS LANE

RAINHAM

BRAMBLE LANE

AVELEY

SOUTH UPMINSTER MANOR

THE EARLY YEARS

Where does one start writing the history of a village? Upminster may not be a village now, but that is what it has been for the greater part of the last thousand years. We must go back to where records began and even try to visualise what the area looked like back in Roman times.

First, let us look at the area we are considering and it is remarkable that the limits of the village going back to the 11th century are almost identical to the parish boundaries of the 1930s, when Upminster became part of the Urban District of Hornchurch. The acreage was about 3,370, the parish being one mile wide and six miles long, north to south. The northern boundary was the River Ingrebourne where it crossed Nag's Head Lane, the river also forming the western boundary where it passed through what is now the Golf Course, past Upminster Bridge and down to Hacton Lane: the line then turned down the Aveley Road to Running Water Wood – the southern extremity – and then northwards along Stubbers Lane, eventually crossing St Mary's Lane at Argyle Gardens, continuing north until Tyler's Common is reached once more. The highest point is in the north on the Common, where the elevation is about 200 feet; from there the terrain slopes gently southwards to only about 50 feet above sea level. The sub-soil in the northern part of the parish is clay, while in the south it is sand and gravel.

'Upminster' has been spelt in various ways over the centuries and there are recorded in local historian Wilson's scrapbooks twenty-four different spellings covering the period from 1086 for the next four hundred years. Wright in his *History of Essex* of 1836 said that the 'Minster' part is Saxon signifying a cathedral or collegiate church, although it sometimes applies to a parish church as in Upminster's case. The addition of

'Up' is considered to relate to its elevated position, although there is much higher land in Upminster than the area of St Laurence's church.

It is fairly certain that settlements existed in the Upminster area as far back as the 1st century. In 1947 fragments of Roman building tiles were found in Running Water Wood and, during the 50s, excavations by the Ministry of Works at South Ockendon Hall discovered a probable burial mound. In a gravel pit at Aveley a sculptured head of the 2nd century was found. The biggest find, though, was in 1937 off Gerpins Lane on the Upminster/Rainham border during gravel excavations. The site was undoubtedly a burial ground and from the finds it is clear that there must have been a settlement in the area from Stone Age times to the 6th century. Discoveries included axe heads, Bronze Age pottery, a gold coin pendant of the 6th century and various items of jewellery of the same period. The most valuable was that of two decorated glass drinking vessels in the shape of cattle horns. These Saxon horns are unique in this country and now reside in the British Museum. In 1948/9 Roman coins and a ring were found in the Brentwood area.

Throughout Essex there are many known Roman roads, the nearest to Upminster being that passing through Romford en route for Colchester. There is no evidence of any Roman roads in the village area, although various notable historians have suggested that there must have been, at least, an east/west trackway. Miller Christy claimed there was a Roman road from Ilford to Bradwell, where the Romans had the fort of Othona, passing through Becontree, Rush Green, Hornchurch and Upminster. A north/south track is even more obscure. Upminster's shape indicates that there should be one road through its six miles north to south length and it is probable that this could have been one of the many pilgrim routes going south through Essex towards Kent and the shrine of Thomas a Beckett in Canterbury.

It looks, therefore, that Upminster did have a community of some sort as far back as recorded English history and, although the settlements were scattered throughout the district, it looks as if the centre was the crossroads where St Laurence Church stands today. This scattered community probably lived in a very wooded area with much waste land and little cultivated acreage.

From the 1st century to the 11th century there is a gap in the records of almost a thousand years, but it is unlikely that changes in the neighbourhood were noticeable from one century to another. The only significant alteration was that in Roman times there was, probably, equality amongst residents, but it is clear from 11th century records that by then there were large landowners and a structured class system for the rest of the villagers. In 1086 William the Conqueror had the census known as the Domesday Book compiled and it is from this that we can once again pick up the history of the parish.

For William the 'Book' was a survey of his new kingdom and its value to him in taxes, but to the villagers it seemed a day of judgement, for many villages had been pillaged and burnt during William's march north after the Conquest.

Essex is rather special, as far as Domesday is concerned, as Essex, Norfolk and Suffolk had far more detailed entries in the Little Domesday Book, than the rest of the country. Even then, Essex was differentiated from the East Anglian counties, as it was Saxon, like Middlesex, Sussex and the Wessex counties. Essex is therefore recorded in hides, which historians think was probably of 120 acres.

Besides recording the situation as it was the surveyors in 1086 also recorded the details of every estate, landowner and peasant in pre-Conquest days and so there is a reference to how things looked twenty years earlier, in 1066. It is fortunate that the survey of Essex was so detailed and, consequently, it can be seen fairly clearly what Upminster looked like in 1066-86 in terms of landowners, the population, the content of the land and the social structure of the times.

The Domesday survey makes mention of three owners of land in Upminster and the entries, as translated in the *Victoria County History of Essex* are -

1. Upmonstra is held by the Holy Cross as $2\frac{1}{2}$ hides and 40 acres. Then 8 villeins, now 6. Then 2 bordars, now 4. Then 4 serfs now 3. Then, as now, 2 ploughs on the demesne and 4 ploughs belonging to the men. Woodland for 300 swine and 6 acres of meadow. There are 2 beasts. Then 20 sheep, now 50. Then 11 swine, now 30.

Then, as now, it was worth 4 pounds. To this manor belongs 1 sokeman with 30 acres and half a plough, and it is worth 20 pence.

2. Upmunstre, which was held by Suen suart as a manor and as $6\frac{1}{2}$ hides and 30 acres, is held by Walter in demesne. Then, as now, 8 villeins. Then 5 bordars, now 7. Then, as now 4 serfs and 2 ploughs on the demesne. Then 5 ploughs belonging to the men, now 4. There is woodland for 200 swine and 8 acres of meadow. Then one colt, now none. There are 110 sheep. It was worth £7, now £8. And there belonged to this manor 10 acres which are held by Geoffrey de "Magnavilla" in exchange, as he says.

3. Upmunstra, which was held by Ulwin as $1\frac{1}{2}$ hides, is held of the Bishop by Mauger. Then two bordars and now the same. Then, as now, one plough. It was worth 20 shillings, now 30 shillings.

The first entry mentioned the Holy Cross as holders of the land and this refers to estates owned by the Canons of the Holy Cross of Waltham (Abbey). Waltham Abbey, therefore, owned about 340 acres in Upminster, the majority in the north of the area, around what is now the Upminster Golf Club.

The second entry refers to land that later became the Manor of Gaynes, occupying much of southern Upminster around the Corbets Tey Road area. This area of $6\frac{1}{2}$ hides and 30 acres totals 810 acres, making it by far the largest Manor in Upminster. At the time of the Conquest it was held by Suen suart, which probably means Suain the Swarthy. He also held a manor at Leyton in the Hundred of Becontree, which was less than half the size of his Upminster property. Suen's father had been Sheriff of Essex under Edward the Confessor, as well as under William. The family had much land both before and after the Conquest, probably due to the French blood in the family. It seems that Suen must have given up Gaynes, probably for a larger estate elsewhere, for the survey noted the land was in the possession of Walter of Douai, who was Flemish and, besides being a great baron in the south-west, held two other Manors in Essex at Rainham (960 acres) and in the Tendring Hundred (780 acres).

The third Upminster manor was in the very south of the parish on the Upminster/Aveley border. This small manor of 180 acres, held by Ulwin in 1066 and Mauger in

1086, formed part of the estates in Essex owned by Bishop Odo of Bayeux, who had 40 Essex manors in all.

A summary of the Domesday findings is –

	Upminster Hall		Gaynes		South Upminster	
	1066	1086	1066	1086	1066	1086
Villeins	8	6	8	8	-	-
Bordars	2	4	5	7	2	2
Serfs	4	3	4	4	-	-
	14	13	17	19	2	2
Ploughs (Manor)	2	2	2	2	1	1
Ploughs (Men)	4	4	5	4	-	-
Woodland	for 300 swine		for 200 swine		-	-
Meadow	6 acres		6 acres		-	-
Beasts	2	2	-	-	-	-
Sheep	20	50	110	110	-	-
Swine	11	30	-	-	-	-
Value p.a.	£4	£4	£7	£8	£1	£1.50
Area	2½ hides, 40 acres		6½ hides, 30 acres		1½ hides	

This census only shows that the working population in 1086 was 34, but, of course, there is no mention of women and children and also we do not know how many people there were in residence at the Manor houses. Presumably there were a few monks at Upminster Hall and probably a family at each of the other two manors. One can only estimate, but possibly the population in 1086 was about 150 or a little more, if the average family had more than two children. The survey lists villeins, bordars and serfs: these were the three classes of peasant, with villeins having more land for themselves – about 30 acres – while serfs held no land at all. Bordars usually had about 5 acres. The *Victoria History* noted that the number of bordars increased over the twenty year period at the expense of the peasant class above and below. It appears, therefore, that in William's reign land became more evenly distributed, giving an average acreage for each peasant of about fifteen. The class above the peasantry were free men or sokenmen, but there do not seem to have been any in the Upminster Manors.

It is difficult to envisage the countryside of the eleventh century, but it is certain that it was very wooded, if the number of swine that grazed is any guide. The *Victoria History* also calculated that the average for the area was 26 swine per 100 acres of woodland: if there was acreage for 500 swine this translates into nearly 2,000 acres of woodland within the total 3,400 acres of Upminster, that is, some 60% of the district was wooded.

An anomaly thrown up by the survey is the number of ploughs used by the Manor and the men on the Upminster Hall and Gaynes manors. The number of ploughs is the same, although one would expect the Gaynes Manor of 810 acres of cultivated soil compared with 300 acres in Upminster Hall to have had many more.

For something like one thousand years, therefore, little had changed in the Upminster area, except the foundation of a church at the old Roman cross-roads, probably in the 7th century. From 1086 the progress of Upminster can be followed through the fortunes of the owners of the two principal manors.

Upminster Hall.

Upminster Hall, about 1920

THE MANORS

Upminster Hall's history in the following three hundred years is little recorded: it must be presumed that peace and contentment reigned and the monks went about their business at the manor with little contact with the other residents of Upminster. A little is known, however, of the history of the formation of the manor as it relates to the Abbey of Waltham Holy Cross.

A wealthy landowner named Tovi, or Tofig, built a church at Waltham to receive a cross which, it was said, was discovered through a vision in Somerset. On Tovi's death his son inherited part of his estate, but lost parts, including Waltham, which Edward the Confessor granted to Earl (later King) Harold Godwinson. Harold enlarged the church, increasing its endowments. The church was dedicated by the Archbishop of York in the presence of King Edward probably in May, 1060. The Abbey was given seventeen manors, mostly in Essex (including Upminster), but some in Surrey, Hertfordshire, Bedfordshire and Berkshire. The King granted a charter in 1062 confirming these manors to the secular church which had been established and this grant was undisturbed by the Conquest. It is noted that after King John's death in 1216 the various manors were ordered to pay rent to Isabel, the Queen Mother, and in 1281 the rent was paid to Queen Eleanor.

The countryside round Upminster being wooded or waste land was subject to continual enclosure as land was brought into use for grazing or agriculture. Up to the time of Richard I in 1190 the King ratified the enclosure of about 100 acres that had been cleared and cultivated by the monks at Upminster Hall. Other minor references do occasionally appear about the manor, but during the 11th to 15th centuries with no changes in ownership there is little to record. The Essex historian, Morant, wrote in 1786 that he felt that Upminster Hall was probably a resting place or hunting lodge for the Abbot of Waltham who would probably bring influential guests for a short stay. The Hall had its own chapel and font – now, incidentally, in St Laurence Church – and the garden seems to have been a cemetary. Champion Branfil took down the chapel and built part of it into the south end of the stables that were destroyed by fire in 1852. Near the stables was a circular arched vault about 25 feet long, that was probably below the chapel: this vault existed until the 1850s. The Upminster historian, Wilson, said that in the 1850s he could remember the ground in the garden sounding hollow and he thought that another vault existed under the garden.

The main structures of the present house are timber and the oldest part is dated about 1450. The staircase and gallery are probably of the time of Charles I. In the immediate location of the house were four ponds, one, in the front of the house and adjacent to Hall Lane was still a pond until the 1960s: it is now a car park. One still exists behind the club house, adjacent to the bowling green; another was at the far end of the field now the miniature golf course; and the last was in the area of Holden Way. This pond, in a small meadow to the east of the manor house, was full of gold and silver fish and was a favourite spot of Champion Branfil, who died in 1790. The pond was surrounded by trees and shrubs and was obviously a very peaceful spot.

Came the Dissolution of the Monasteries and, in 1540, Upminster Hall changed hands and it was granted, amongst other estates, to Thomas Cromwell, the Lord Privy Seal, who was Henry VIII's right-hand man at this time.

When Cromwell, by now Earl of Essex, was beheaded in 1543, Upminster Hall reverted to the King, who sold it that August to Ralph Latham, who purchased Gaynes that same year. Ralph was the son of Robert Latham of North Ockendon, other branches of the family coming from Stifford and Aveley. Ralph died on 19th July, 1557, leaving Upminster Hall to his son, William, who leased it (and Gaynes) to William Strangman, William Wiseman and others. Wiseman's name is recorded in the Essex Quarter Sessions Rolls of Recusants in June, 1586, for not attending church for the previous seven years and for not receiving the sacraments.

Upminster Hall was purchased in 1642 by Juliana, Viscountess Dowager Campden, for £6,640. It had been in the Latham family for 99 years. After Lady Campden's death the property passed to other members of her family, the last being the Earl of Gainsborough. The Earl sold the Manor in 1685 to Captain Andrew Branfil, who was a sea captain hailing from Dartmouth. He died in 1709 at the age of 69, when Champion Branfil succeeded to the estate at the age of 26. Champion was High Sheriff of Essex in 1736 and he died in 1738.

His son and heir, Champion, was born in 1712 and was also 26 when he inherited the Manor and estate. He was a barrister and died in 1770, being succeeded by his son, Champion, who was born in 1764. This Champion died, aged 28, in 1792, when his son, Champion Edward, was only three. At that time the family were living at Canterbury, where his father died and Champion Edward was born. He died in 1844 and the estate passed to his widow Mrs. Ann Eliza Branfil. Mrs. Branfil died in 1873, when her second son, Col. Benjamin Aylett Branfil, became Lord of the Manor and owner of Upminster Hall. Benjamin's heir was his grandson, Champion Andrew, the last of the Branfil's to hold the estate, much of which had been sold by 1906 to W P Griggs (later Upminster Estates, Ltd.). In 1921 the remainder was sold to Godfrey Pike, who, in 1927, sold this estate and the lordship separately. The latter was sold to Upminster Estates and eventually bought from the company in 1938 by Essex County Council. The estate was bought by the South Essex Brick and Tile Company which, in 1927, leased the Hall itself and $6\frac{1}{2}$ acres to the Upminster Golf Club, which acquired the freehold in 1935.

Upminster Hall, therefore, had only a few changes of family ownership in the four hundred years from the Dissolution of the Monasteries until twentieth century development: Gaynes, on the other hand, had a more chequered career.

The Gaynes Manor passed from Walter of Douai (of 1086) to the hands of the Fitzurse family in the twelfth century. Richard Fitzurse was a notable figure in English history at the time Stephen was King between 1135 and 1154, being captured with Stephen at Lincoln in 1140 by the Empress Maud's forces. The Fitzurse family was still active in politics a few years later when Reginald, son of Richard and Lord of the Manor, struck the first blow at the Canterbury murder of Thomas a Beckett.

The Manor then passed through other members of the Fitzurse family until it was acquired by rather devious means by Vitalis Engayne, a great-grandson of Richard Fitzurse. Thus the first Engayne came on the scene in 1218 and it is from this family that the estate took its name.

Vitalis died in 1244 and the manor passed, via his son, Henry, to his younger brother John, who became Sir John in later years. Sir John built an extra chapel on the north side of the church, called the Engayne Chapel, towards the end of the thirteenth century as a family burial place. The first Sir John died in 1297 and the next two owners were also Sir John Engaynes, the latter going to France with Edward III during the Hundred Years' War, collecting various honours for service in the field.

The last Engayne to hold Gaynes was Sir Thomas, who died in 1367, at which time the family estates in central and south-east England were broken up. It appears that, when the first Sir John died, the following members of the family held Gaynes as tenants in chief, with the Havering family as lessees. The manor passed first to Simon de Havering, then to John de Havering and from him to his wife, who eventually died in 1393. Then the manor passed to the Deyncourt family, although it seems that Lora de Havering had the right to live at the manor until her death.

Sir John Deyncourt inherited Gaynes through the hand of the King, but, sadly, he also died in 1393 leaving only a son, Roger, who was a minor and who, therefore, became a ward of the King with the monarch having the right to grant the manor to whoever he wished until Roger came of age.

At this stage we must go back a few years to mention another notable person who became involved in Upminster's history. Edward III was captivated by Alice Perrers, who was in the service of Queen Philippa. The King lavished gifts of money and land on Alice and she very soon became a powerful woman in the realm, even to the extent of influencing the law of the land to her own ends. Parliament soon got fed up with her antics and passed a law forbidding women to practise in the courts. She was banished for a short period and, following the King's death in 1377, returned, having married Sir William Windsore, Deputy of Ireland. In 1380 Sir William supported Richard II in his war with France and for his services was granted all the lands Alice had held as a single woman, including many estates in the London area as well as the Manor of Upminster (as Gaynes was then known).

Now two parties seemed to have the rights to the Manor. Roger Deyncourt should have inherited it at his majority, but Richard II was giving the manor to Sir William Windsore.

It seems that Alice Perrers did live at Gaynes for some time whilst Roger was a minor, until her death in 1400: she was buried in St Laurence Church. In her will she left Gaynes to her younger daughter Joan and to her elder daughter Jane she left her other manors, with a request that they both recover from John Windsore, her husband's nephew, all the property that he allegedly acquired illegally. In 1406 Joan asked the King to release the manor to her as her mother's heir, and it was decided that an enquiry should be held. That November a judgement was made that Joan, now married, should surrender Gaynes for an annual settlement for life. The settlement also entailed giving up a property called Godehous in Upminster, which was later known as Goodhouse and, later still, as Harold Court.

Following Joan's departure and Roger Deyncourt becoming the rightful owner of the estate the De la Feld family were tenants at Gaynes. By good fortune the De la Feld daughter married Roger Deyncourt, bringing the whole matter full circle and the Deyncourt family back to Gaynes. The whole problem was finally resolved in 1419 when the King (now Henry V) formally recognised Roger Deyncourt as the owner and the King's hand was finally removed from Gaynes, meaning that the estate was held freehold by Roger with no strings attached.

Roger died in 1455 and the estate passed through his son, Robert, to his grand-daughter, Ellyn, who married Nicholas Wayte, a London draper. It is at this time that the new rich emerged as owners of manors: the merchants and the professional people gradually took over the estates previously owned by farming barons. Both Nicholas Wayte and his wife died within a couple of years of each other in the 1540s and, as they had no children, the estate was inherited by John Pyke, who was husband of a near relative, Agnes Wayte. John Pyke almost immediately sold the estate to Ralph Latham, a London goldsmith. It is interesting to note that the estate then comprised 1,000 acres, although part was in Hornchurch. The estate thus comprised almost a third of Upminster's area, but in the previous 450 years (from 1086) the size of the estate had fallen considerably.

It has previously been noted that Upminster Hall Manor was bought by Ralph Latham in 1543, so now the situation was that for the first time in history one man owned the majority of Upminster village. Apart from the two large manors the remaining acreage owned by others was very small.

Following Ralph's death his son, William, who had married Anne Strangman of Hadleigh, inherited both manors. The Lord of the Manor had his own pew in the church and, as the most important member of the community, was expected to occupy that pew for Sunday services. Apparently the pew was invariably left empty, which did not please William Washer, the current incumbent. Mrs Latham seems to have been the main offender and William was summoned before the Archdeacon's Court to explain his wife's continual absence from church. The feud with the church did not end there for, in later years, there are records of disputes over tithes and also the rather more serious case of an affray in the church during a service. As the Latham pew had been left empty for so long someone else was occupying it and, although this would not appear important for a non-church-going family, there was some prestige in the position of one's pew in the church. On one occasion when the pew was occupied by another family three of Latham's servants who were in the church at the time took the pew back by force during the service. A few months after that incident William Latham died, in May, 1600.

The records now become unclear. During William's life he leased the manor or the lands to various friends or relatives, before it all eventually came back into his own occupancy. William's son, also a William, died in 1614, passing the manors to his son, another Ralph, who was a lawyer and a Common Sergeant of the City of London. This Ralph disposed of Gaynes, choosing to live at New Place. The Court Rolls for the Manor are deposited at the Essex Record Office, but, sadly, that part is missing covering the period when the Latham family ended its association with Gaynes. Upminster Hall manor had passed out of the Latham family in 1642, but probably Gaynes was sold some time earlier.

The Herbert family were the next owners, who sold it to the Graves family, who held the manor for sixty years. Joseph Graves' widow decided to sell in 1722 and correspondence between her solicitor and Sir Nathan Wright, a prospective purchaser, revealed that he thought it worth £2,500. The rental income of the estate at the time was £88, but Sir Nathan, who owned Cranham Hall, did not buy the estate and it was sold to Amos White of whom nothing is known. The manor was then sold to George Montgomery in 1749. Montgomery came from the county of the same name and had purchased a few years earlier an estate at Bowers Gifford. Montgomery had one of the few maps of his estate drawn up, showing the house and grounds and immediate fields with their names. The house was off Little Gaynes Lane at, roughly, the bottom of Gaynes Court, today a small cul-de-sac extending towards Tawney Avenue. A second map, drawn at the same time, showed the full extent of the manor, incorporating Stubbers in the extreme south, Hactons in Hacton Lane and New Place, which was where New Place Gardens is today, off St Mary's Lane. Following Montgomery's death his trustees looked after the estate for some years before the manor was acquired by Sir James Esdaile.

James Esdaile was the grandson of Baron d'Estaile, a French nobleman who fled France at the time of Louis XIV and came to live in England. James' father was a rich merchant and his son inherited his flair for trade, soon becoming rich himself and, like other merchants of that time, moving into the property market. The Esdailes were originally leaseholders on the Gaynes estate, probably at Hoppy Hall, which was opposite Springfield Gardens where the GPO sorting office and petrol filling

Sir James Esdaile   by permission of Sabin Galleries

station now stand. It was about 1748 when he moved to Upminster with his wife and two children, Peter and Louise. His wife died and he married Mary Mayor, who had inherited New Place, also part of the Gaynes estate, from her father, John, also a London merchant. James Esdaile prospered and became Sheriff of London and Middlesex in 1766. He got his knighthood the same year for his address to King George III on the occasion of the birth of his third daughter, Charlotte, and also the marriage of the King's sister, Caroline, to King Christian IV of Denmark. Four years later he acquired the Manor of Gaynes and, with his wealth, was able to start a building programme that included a new Gaynes manor house, New Place, Harwood Hall, Londons, Gaynes Lodge and various other small houses. Of these, Harwood Hall and Gaynes Lodge still stand today. The effect of this activity was to develop the southern end of Upminster, which, in turn, increased the population of the village due to the number of servants and the tradesmen needed to service them.

It is unfortunate that no drawings exist of the great mansion that was built for the Esdailes by James Paine, who was a leading architect of the day. His designs include Thordon Hall, which he did for the 9th Lord Petre in 1764, and it is quite possible that Gaynes had a similar appearance. The only description of the manor is dated 1856, which was after it was demolished, and this described the building as having had a central mansion with two linked wings. It had a lofty portico in the Corinthian order approached by winding steps on either side. As the main floor was elevated this gave splendid views of the estate southwards. The rooms were described as elegant, rather than large, with the whole interior in keeping with the requirements of a manorial residence of that age.

Between 1770 and Esdaile's death in 1793, the population grew with villagers building small properties on the waste land between the highway and the fields. Roadways at that time were very wide and it was possible to build a cottage on the waste land without encroaching on the land belonging to the manor or a freeholder. The population of Upminster in 1770 was about 550/600, but by the Census of 1801 it had risen to 765. Incidentally, the parish of Cranham then had a population of only about 240.

Sir James, besides his secular building projects also rebuilt the old Lady Chapel in Upminster Church. A tablet commemorating this is still in the church. Another tablet tells the story of one of Sir James' sons, James. This James had seven sons, but, tragically, two of his sons, John and Peter, died within a week of each other in May, 1802, at the ages of 20 and 19 respectively: the third death was one of his daughters, Susanna, who died three years later aged eighteen. These family deaths obviously had a long lasting effect on James for, in 1812, he was found shot in the grounds of New Place, whilst his carriage was being brought to the front door for a business trip to London. There seems little doubt that it was suicide brought about through grief for his family losses, but there are no records to prove this point. James' widow placed a memorial plaque in the church over the Esdaile vault. It says:

"He was a firm, serious and pious Christian and his religious principles were not more conspicuously exemplified in the candour and liberality of his sentiments than in the charity and beneficience of his actions.

"He died sincerely and deservedly lamented by all who knew him, particularly by the poor of the neighbourhood where he resided, but most poignantly by his mourning widow and children to whom his loss is irreparable. Yet they mourn not as those who have no hope, they confidently and piously rely on the gracious promises of him, who in the sacred words of Revelation hath declared that 'As in Adam all die, even so in Christ shall all be made alive.' He died on the 16th day of January, in the 60th year of his age."

On the death of Sir James in 1793 his son, Peter, inherited Gaynes and lived there until his death in 1817 at the age of 74. Peter did not have any children and so the manor and estate passed to James, the eldest son of the James who committed suicide. The large estate that the Esdailes had built up was shortlived for, less than fifty years after the first James acquired Gaynes, the estate was broken up. In 1817 the stock was sold and two years later the estate was up for sale in lots.

At the first sale only a part of the estate was

sold. A second sale in 1820 tried to sell the manor house in lots with the exception of the eastern wing. The park and land immediately adjoining the manor house, together with the remaining wing and all the outbuildings, were sold in seven lots and bought by local residents. All but the east wing was demolished and, like the large estate, the manor house only lasted 50 years.

In 1821 the Rev. John Clayton built Gaynes Villa on a plot he had purchased a little to the left of the original mansion. The still-standing east wing was occupied by Clayton's daughter and son-in-law (Mr and Mrs Johnson). The manor, what was left of it, and New Place still belonged to James Esdaile Junior. The Esdailes retained their interest in Upminster for a further 20 years until, in 1839, New Place was sold for £4,900 to James Harmer, a London Alderman, and the manor with its rights was sold to James Cudden of Norwich for only £810. Other properties on the estate and the sum they realised were High House, Corbets Tey, £880; West Lodge, Corbets Tey Road, £520; and Hunts Farm (at the corner of Springfield Gardens), £7,800. The last remaining estate property was the Bell Inn which was sold to Mr F Seabrook for £3,200 in 1886.

When Rev. Clayton of the new Gaynes Villa died his son, who was also in the church, inherited the property. Mr & Mrs Johnson moved out of the East Wing and the last part of the largest Gaynes Manor on the site was pulled down. George Clayton built a new Gaynes in 1846, which lasted eighty years until it was demolished in the modern development of Upminster. The Rev George died in 1862 and his widow married Henry Joslin. On her death the estate was sold to H A Gilliat in 1874, who in that year also bought Londons Farm of 52 acres. Gilliat tried to set up a large scale dairy farm, but this venture failed and, in 1878, he sold the estate to Henry Joslin. Joslin followed in Esdaile's footsteps by building up the Gaynes estate again with the purchase of Hoppy Hall farm of 98 acres and, in 1890, he bought Hunts Farm of 130 acres back into the estate. Following Joslin's death in 1927 Gaynes manor house was again demolished and the whole estate was broken up and sold for building land.

The catalogue for the sale of Gaynes estate in 1928 is held at the Essex Record Office [ref.A.314], as are the books containing the details of the Manor Court for the period 1678-1934. The catalogue shows that the estate had been reduced to only 400 acres by the time of the sale, the majority of that acreage being Gaynes itself (105 acres), Hoppy Hall farm (94 acres) and Hunts Farm (130 acres). A hundred years earlier, in the times of the Esdailes, the acreage was 3,000, although this included land in Dagenham and Cranham. The 1928 sale broke these remaining 400 acres into 17 lots, some of which were very small, being just properties without farm land. Hoppy Hall, Hunts, Londons and various cottages were all sold without the accompanying farm land which was sold off as parcels of building land of up to 80 acres.

For example, Lot 2 was 61 acres of building land encompassing the area now occupied by Tawney Avenue, Corbets Tey Road, Parkland Avenue and Hacton Lane. Another parcel of building land off Corbets Tey Road was half of Hunts Farm, some 68 acres extending from where Springfield Gardens is now to Park Drive. The second part of Hunts was 81 acres, starting at Park Drive and extending to Cranston Park Avenue. And so the 17 lots were sold and one by one the old buildings came down, although Tadlows still stands, as does Gaynes Lodge - the property at the junction of Little Gaynes Lane and Corbets Tey Road. Londons lasted until 1965 and was where Londons Close is sited on the way to Corbets Tey village. All that remains of Gaynes mansion itself is part of the garden walls which have been used as boundary walls for some of the properties in Little Gaynes Gardens and Gaynes Court. Parklands Open Space, with the lake and the bridge, are all that remains of the spacious grounds of that once large country estate.

THE OLD BUILDINGS

Two principal buildings have already been noted - the manor houses of Upminster Hall and Gaynes - as have, briefly, other properties owned from time to time by the lords of the manor. There are or were, of course, other historic buildings in the village: some of the existing roads and land-marks are referred to below for ease of identification.

Starting at the western side of the parish in St Mary's Lane at the bottom of Upminster Hill, where the road crosses the River Ingrebourne. In the early nineteenth century the bridge there was wooden and only eleven feet wide with only light traffic allowed to use it, while heavy carts and stagecoaches had to cross ten yards further downstream by way of a ford. Here, on land now occupied by Hornchurch Stadium, stood Bridge House or Bridge House Farm or Briggehous, as it was in the Middle Ages. Bridge House was a manor, but it was not mentioned in Domesday and did not grow to any size until the 14th century: it was not a real manor, like Upminster Hall or Gaynes, as it did not have a manor court. The earliest record of the property was in 1375 when John de Reydon passed the manor to John Cook. In 1419 it was held by Joane, widow of Roger Ashburnham, for the annual payment of a pound of wax. The manor owned the land directly around the building on the south side, together with 23 acres on the north side of Upminster Hill, extending from the river up the hill to Station Road. In addition the farm rented land in the 15th century from the manor of Dovers in Hornchurch (30 acres) and a further 18 acres from the manor of Gidea Hall, Romford. 66 acres of pasture and woodland were rented from the Warden and Fellows of New College, Oxford, on the Hornchurch side of the Ingrebourne. The estate changed hands later in the 15th century, for in the reign of Edward IV state papers of the Close Rolls record that an indenture was signed in 1479 between Robert Plomer and John Godstone in respect of a tenement called Briggehous and other lands covenanting that if "John Godstone pay to the aforesaid Robert Plomer or his heirs £80 sterling then the said Robert Plomer shall make a lawful estate of the above lands to the said John Godstone". Later in the century the manor was merged with Gaynes and in the ownership of the Deyncourt and Latham families. The property was subsequently sold to the Wright family of Cranham Hall and, in 1727, it was sold to Thomas Harding Newman of Hornchurch. Richard Newman of Nelmes Manor, Hornchurch, was the owner in 1800 and he later sold the farm to the Nokes family who built the windmill in 1802/3. Up to that time the farm was some way from the road, possibly 50 yards back, but, following a sale to the Emanuel family, who were London jewellers, a new farm house was built in 1850 much closer to the road. In 1899 the Wills tobacco family owned the property in the name of Sir Edward Payson Wills. Following its purchase in 1910 by Edward Battson, the estate was quickly broken up for residential development. A conveyance of 1912 shows the farm as having about 32 acres extending over an area now occupied by the Stadium along to Bridge Avenue and back as far as Southview Drive.

Opposite Bridge Avenue at the bottom of Upminster Hill on the north side are a row of dwellings called Ingrebourne Cottages. This was the parish workhouse built in 1750 to house the poor of Upminster. Each parish was responsible for its own poor and, in the 18th century, parishioners met in the church vestry to discuss local matters, including the welfare of the poor. The Vestry, as the body came to be known, administered the poor relief which was collected from local residents as part of the annual rates. Records show that Upminster's yearly expenditure on the poor exceeded £100 in 1740 and had risen to £860 by 1800. The expenditure peaked at £1,200 in 1802, falling to between £600 and £900 until 1836, when the poor were transferred to Romford. Well before the poor house was built there had been a fund for their care, usually through the church and the poor box. Village orphans were apprenticed to local craftsmen and lodged out in the village at the expense of the poor fund. Part of the finance for the building of the workhouse came from the sale of stock held by trustees for the poor. A Vestry meeting on 2nd November, 1749, chaired by the Rev. Samuel Bradshaw resolved -

"It is this day ordered and agreed that a house shall forthwith be built for the use of the poor and that £110, now in South Sea Annuities at 4%, be employed for building the same and that the parishioners do continue to pay annually the interest of the same to the poor as has been done, and that those whose names are underwritten do take care to carry on the said building."

Up to the time of the building there were about eighteen people lodged out in the village, but the new Poor House could not take them all. In 1762 the inmates totalled ten, of whom six were widows and the rest probably orphans. By the 1780s the problem of the poor was increasing and there was a need for more accommodation, as some were being lodged in the Great Warley workhouse. In May, 1783, the Vestry Minutes resolved -

"It was resolved that it is necessary to make an additional building to the present Workhouse and that the Churchwardens and Overseers be desired to apply to the Lord of the Manor of Upminster to enclose part of the waste adjoining to the Workhouse for the purpose of making additional rooms, yard, etc. to the present Workhouse."

The roadside waste was owned by the Lord of the Manor, but, although no record exists of the granting of permission to build the original workhouse, the Manor Rolls of 1784 do record a grant of land -

"At a Court Baron of Champion Branfill Lord of the Manor of Upminster Hall before Jonah Beckwith Gentleman Steward there, a grant was made to the Churchwardens of Upminster of a piece of ground part of the waste soil of the manor situated near the Bridge in the highway between Upminster and Hornchurch (25½ rods by 2½ rods) and the messuage standing thereon for the use of the inhabitants of Upminster as a Workhouse for the poor at a yearly rent of 2/6 [12½p] paid every year on the Feast Day of St Michael the Archangel."

By 1786 the extension was complete and, from the Overseer's accounts, it appears that the four poor who had been at the Warley workhouse were transferred to Upminster. The highest number of inmates recorded was 37 in 1803, when the workhouse master put in a claim for allowances.

When the workhouse was built in 1759 there was probably no paid master appointed and the house was run by the paupers themselves. In 1761 the Vestry Minutes recommend that someone be appointed "to take care of the children and other poor as shall be brought into the said workhouse". There were various Masters and Mistresses, including Mrs Elizabeth Clark, who succeeded her husband as Mistress when he died and who claimed £9.13.6d for four weeks for 28 inmates, not much per pauper even in those days. The Masters or Mistresses received a wage for their duties – in 1789 John Smith had, in addition to his five shillings a week wage, 2/6d in the pound of the earnings of the paupers. The latter were employed in basket and rope making, spinning and weaving, and the income went towards their upkeep, less any commission paid to the Master. In 1833 the allowance per inmate to the Master for their care was 3/6d [17½p] a week.

Parish workhouses were abolished in 1834, when the Poor Law Amendment Act was passed. Parishes were grouped into Unions and, in this case it was Romford that became responsible for Upminster's poor. In 1836 the old workhouse was sold to George Rowe for £356.12.5d and the fixtures were sold for £31.7.6d. The monies were passed to the Romford Union towards the building of a new workhouse at Oldchurch. The property was converted into six tenement cottages by Rowe and the main structure stands today as it was in 1786, following the extension to the property. The rent was still payable to the manor and this continued up until 1906, when it was redeemed by a lump sum of £3.3.6d. Looking at the building todays it does not look much in terms of appearance or structural interest, but from 1750 to 1834 it played a very important part in the lives of many residents of Upminster, both as a home for many of the poor and for the problems of administration by the principal residents of the village.

Moving up Upminster Hill, the next notable building was 'Red House'. For those who have lived in Upminster for some time this will be remembered as the Drill Hall where the Territorial Army had its local headquarters from 1930. It was situated on the south side of the hill where Tyrells Close is now. This Georgian house was built in 1795 by Samuel Hammond, the local builder and carpenter, for William Watson, a solicitor. It was one of the minor houses of Upminster and did not play any great part in the history of the village.

On both sides of the road up Upminster Hill from the River Ingrebourne to the Windmill the land immediately at the roadside was waste land. Apart from the workhouse land, it appears that at the end of the 18th century all this land was granted to the parish by the manor of Upminster Hall, which owned the north side, and by the manor of Gaynes, the south.

Just past Red House on the way up the Hill were nine tenement cottages, one of which was a beerhouse, also built on land owned by Samuel Hammond. These were built in the 1780s and stood until 1908, when they were pulled down in a very dilapidated condition. The land where they stood was then in the ownership of Sir Edward Wills of Bridge House.

The only other property on the workhouse side of the road was Ivy Cottage, also built on waste land in 1792. Shoes for the workhouse were made here by Elizabeth Murduck.

Back on the south side, past the Red House and the cottages, the next property uphill was Minster House, also known as Upminster House and Hill House. This was another of Samuel Hammond's constructions of 1792 and was built for Mrs Elizabeth Fries as a girls' school and continued as such until 1915, when it changed to a private mixed school. The site of the school, demolished in 1963, is the plot of empty land alongside the Old Chapel. This Chapel was, of course, built by Samuel Hammond, at a cost of less than £500 in 1800. The freehold was bought from Gaynes manor in 1803 for £23, plus expenses. The chapel was the Congregational Church until 1911, when they had their new church built in Station Road, the old chapel being sold to the Plymouth Brethren for £400.

At the crown of the Hill is Hill Place, now the girls' convent school. There was, though, in its present grounds a house on the road frontage, just about where the school entrance is now. This was a private boys' school run by Thomas Talbot, registered in the Bishop's Court by Henry Asley, Minister, on 22nd December, 1794. The Congregational Church bought the property in 1847 for £250, as a residence for its pastors of the chapel. In 1872 Mr Temple Soanes of Hill Place purchased the site and a plot on the other side of the road. The old house was pulled down and a new manse built opposite in 1873: this manse lasted until 1935 when it was pulled down for residential development.

Hill Place was built in 1790 and was originally part of Sir James Esdaile's Gaynes estate. In 1827 it was owned by a Romford solicitor, Wasey Sterry, and following his death was let to a succession of tenants before being bought by Temple Soanes in 1867. One of these tenants was the well-known horticulturist, Miss Ellen Willmott of Warley Place, who added her own touch during her stay by transforming 20 acres on the north side of St Mary's Lane, previously belonging to the mill property, into a well wooded paddock of plants, various shrubs and trees. The whole estate, in about 1860, occupied 32 acres with 12 acres surrounding the house on the south side of Upminster Hill.

Soanes commissioned William Gibbs Bartlett, who had previously redesigned the parish church, to reconstruct Hill Place in the Gothic style still seen today. In 1895 the house was bought by E S Woodiwiss, who kept a private zoo in the grounds and who had the honour of welcoming to his house the cricketer, W G Grace, when he visited Upminster in 1896. Three years later Sir E P Wills, who bought Bridge House Farm the same year, purchased Hill Place. A subsequent owner was Dr Brookfield and the house was bought in 1927 by the Order of the Sacred Heart as a convent and Catholic girls' school. A previous sale of the property in 1902 described the house as having an entrance hall with marble and oak panelling, two drawing rooms, a dining room, a billiard room and servants' quarters. On the upper floor were 15 bedrooms and two bathrooms. The outbuildings were three loose horseboxes, four stalls, a coach house, grooms' rooms and a lodge. The grounds, which have changed little since, comprised eleven acres of lawns and shrubberies, although when Wilson wrote his *History and Topography of Upminster* in 1881, he described the property as having 32 acres. Hill Place was obviously very large and one of the main properties of the village. Following its conversion to a school a new wing was built in 1930 and the chapel was added in 1935. At the outbreak of war in 1939 the school closed and was transferred as a complete unit to Chilton House, Buckinghamshire. During the war it was occupied by the army, but in 1946 the school moved back and it reopened as a day and boarding school, but under the auspices of the local Education Authority.

Continuing to the crossroads there are three buildings of note. The Church and the Windmill will be considered later, but the Rectory was built in 1765 on the site of an earlier rectory that had a moat. Forty yards of the moat remained on the north side of St Mary's Lane until 1810 and there was a small piece still visible in the 1850s in the southwest corner of the lawn. The rectory is still standing today, although now used as offices, but it is the same building built for the Rev Samuel Bradshaw. The Glebe land (belonging to the church for the benefit of the clergy) extended for 22 acres along Corbets Tey Road and is now the playing fields. There was once a spacious tithe barn on the glebe and Dr William Derham, rector from 1689 to 1735, planted many trees that survived until Dutch Elm Disease killed many in the early 1980s.

At the crossroads, which has changed a lot since the 1750s, stood 'The Bell'. There is a fairly well-founded theory that Upminster had a traditional village pond and stocks at this site. The pond existed until about 1800, while the stocks were removed in 1814. The original 'Bell' inn was some 40 yards southeast of the 'Bell' that older residents remember, probably on the edge of the circular village green. There is no record of when the first inn was built, but it must have been some time before 1636 when Elizabeth Saward was the landlord. Opposite the 'Bell' in Corbets Tey Road stands the Church, again well back from the road and, although the ground abutting the present crossroads is now a graveyard, back in the 18th century it was open meadow and probably not fenced. Wilson, in his scrapbooks, mentions a map of Upminster dated 1720, although no trace of this map has been found. Wilson says that in that year there were twelve buildings at the village centre, apart from the Church, one of which was at the top of the alley which is the small path between what is now the Woolwich Building Society and the new development of shops and flats in St Mary's Lane. Once again, with this Wilson reference, it can be seen that the buildings were all back from the present building line. The remaining corner is that bounded by Station Road and St Mary's Lane east. Until 1957, just in front of Lloyd's Bank, stood the Cosy Corner cottage. This small property was built in 1831 by Samuel Hammond on a piece of unenclosed village green, according to Wilson. This part of the green belonged to Upminster Hall, whereas the 'Bell' site was in the manor of Gaynes.

The old 'Bell' was pulled down by Sir James Esdaile and the new 'Bell' was built in 1770. From then onwards other buildings encroached on to the old village green and the Church enclosed its small meadow, so that the formation of the modern crossroads can be distinguished, although even well into the 19th century the cross road was very wide, as can be demonstrated by the 1842 map of Upminster drawn up by the Tithe Commission of England and Wales in connection with the allocation of rent charge in lieu of tithes [Essex Record Office, Chelmsford, D/CT 373A plus map]. The map is in very large scale, naming the owners and tenants of all the properties in the parish with total acreage. At that time there were only 65 landowners in Upminster, which means that, out of the 200 or so houses, the majority were rented. The adult population at this time was about 1,100. The map shows the land in front of the Church as the Rectory Meadow and enclosed by this time. Opposite stood the 'Bell', still owned by the Esdailes of Gaynes, with Thomas Clarke as the tenant publican. Besides the inn on the Corbets Tey Road side (where Shoppers' Paradise is now) was the pub yard and, for those that can remember that yard, where the 86A buses turned round up to the 1950s, there was a pond at the time of the map. In Wilson's first book on Upminster he mentioned that in 1856 there were two annual fairs held in Upminster, one at Corbets Tey on the second Friday in July and the other in front of the 'Bell' on Whit Tuesday, which he describes as "A sober affair of toys, nuts and gingerbread".

Crossing diagonally from the 'Bell' site to the Alley, I can still recall visiting an old relation in the 1940s in one of the cottages at the top of that alley, which later became part of Aggis's workshop. The enclosure of the village green had meant that houses were built in front of the Avenue Cottages, as they were called. Where the recent development has taken place on the west side of the Alley, there were some cottages; originally one of these housed the village Post Office, which had been transferred from another cottage in Corbets Tey Road, where Woolworth's is now. At the time of the 1842 survey these were owned by Samuel Hammond, as were all the other properties on this side of the crossroads, including the Avenue Cottages. On the Woolwich Building Society corner site stood Locksley Villa and Chestnuts. The former was a detached red brick house, set well back from the road with a long garden: it was demolished in 1936. Chestnuts was named after the very large trees that stood in its front garden, the house looking like a farmhouse, also well set back from the road. It was pulled down in 1935. At the time of the sale the site was owned by the Aggis family, who used the land for their garage business, the Chestnuts Garage continuing until 1980. The garage site itself was also owned by Samuel Hammond, who, although not one of the principal landowners in terms of acreage in 1842, owned the freehold of land that today is very valuable.

It is worth digressing at this stage to examine Samuel Hammond and his business. Samuel Hammond senior lived from 1746 to 1826 and lived at West Lodge, Corbets Tey Road [which is now the Country Club set behind the shops]. He had two sons, Samuel and William, whose life spans were 1779-1851 and 1787-1862 respectively. Hammond senior was the village contractor who could turn his hand from the simplest carpentry job to the building of new properties in the district. He was the builder of Red House, Minster House, the Old Chapel and many cottages, as well as the parish workhouse where he built the extension in 1786 at a cost of £180. In 1803 he added a loom shed where the paupers spun wool and flax, the cost of this being £64.10s.0d. Hammond's name appears again in connection with the workhouse with regard to the supply of water. Originally the workhouse had no water supply of its own and it was proposed at a Vestry meeting that a well be sunk for this purpose. The proposal was rejected and a counter proposal made by James Esdaile that Mr Hammond be paid four guineas a year for the use of the pump in his yard at the 'Bell' corner. It was also suggested that a barrow be supplied to the workhouse for the carrying of the water from the yard down the hill. The scene of a couple of pauper boys pushing a barrow with an empty barrel up the hill can be easily imagined. On the way back the barrel would, of course, be full and with the weight of the water they must have lost control on many an occasion – only to have to return to the yard for a refill!

Samuel Hammond was a member of St Laurence Church and in 1782 he was Treasurer of the Church Singing Society. The Church gave the Society an allowance of £2.2.0d a year for the purchasing of psalm books, music paper, etc. Samuel was an obvious man for church repairs and, from the Churchwardens' accounts, it is clear that the family undertook minor and major repairs to the fabric. In 1800 Samuel did repairs to the steeple that cost £56.2.2$\frac{1}{4}$d. The church tower had four bells until unfortunately one of Hammond's workmen dropped a large piece of timber on one, cracking it so as to render it useless. The bell was sold and the church made do with only three bells for many years after.

The maintenance of roads and bridges was the responsibility of the parish and, in Upminster's case, there were two surveyors appointed to look after the roads and bridges in the north and south of the parish. Hammond's firm was used for repair work and, in particular, the bridge over the Ingrebourne at the bottom of Upminster Hill required a fair amount of the contractor's attention. In 1782 a resolution by the gentlemen of the Vestry to build a stone bridge was contested and repairs were made with timber. This turned out to be an unwise decision, as Hammond's firm was called on various occasions in succeeding years to make additional repairs costing nearly £200, whereas the cost of a new stone bridge would have been only £220 in 1782. Another bridge that was Upminster's responsibility was one in the extreme northwest of the parish where the road from Warley meets the Ardleigh Green Road at the bottom of Shepherd's Hill. This also crossed the Ingrebourne and was known as Cockleborne or Cockabourne Bridge. Unlike the Upminster Hill Bridge the parish paid Hammond to build a brick bridge in 1790 and this lasted until 1892 when it was taken over by Essex County Council. In 1813 Hammond renewed the railing around the pond at the 'Bell' at a cost of £11.9.5d.

Returning to the older properties of the village, Station Road, which was still called Hall Lane until the railway came, had on the left hand side two cottages with an orchard behind, together with a bakehouse. These were built in 1802 and survived until 1953 when they were pulled down for Essex House to be built. The cottages were owned by Thomas Nokes, the owner of the Windmill and were let to sundry occupants. The last baker was the Abraham family, whose full story is associated with the Windmill, but older residents will not complain to be reminded of Abraham's bakery as one of the last remnants of old Upminster. Even in the late 1940s one could buy a penny [a real penny!] loaf – a little mini-loaf about four inches long – that came very hot and crusty straight from the oven. On Saturdays the cockle and whelk man stood with his wicker basket outside the shop by the Station Road pavement.

On the other side of the road was the Cosy Corner. In 1842 this was a butcher's with living accommodation above. William Hammond then owned the property. Next door was a small farm building and garden. Champion E Branfil of Upminster Hall owned the land and Joseph Lee was the tenant. Joseph was for a long time the publican of the 'Bell' and, after retiring in 1823, he lived at Oak Place, which was a cottage opposite the International Stores in St Mary's Lane. It is probable that Joseph leased the Hall Lane farm as a small market garden when he was running the 'Bell'. In 1848 Mrs Branfil gave part of the land that Lee rented to the Parish so that a school could be built and, on the site where the National Westminster Bank stands today, there was the National School for Boys. This was opened in March, 1851, but one month earlier the British School for Girls had been opened across the road.

The Essex Herald of 17 June, 1853, records that the children of the British School, after their examinations, had gone to the grounds of Gaynes Manor to commemorate the Jubilee Year of the British & Foreign Bible Society. Under an extensive marquee, erected in front of the house, a large lunch of beef and plum puddings and numerous extras was provided for 150 children, including those that had recently left. After the lunch a meeting was held, with the appropriate speeches being made by ministers and the local gentry. Every child received a medal, struck by the Rev George Clayton, to commemorate the Jubilee. The medal was the size of a ten pence piece, having on one side an open Bible supported by a dove bearing an olive branch and surrounded with the inscription 'Truth, Liberty and Love'. On the reverse was the date '1863' and 'Bible Society Jubilee'. Sports followed the presentation and after that tea was provided for the children, their friends and relations, totalling between five and six hundred.

The National School, in later years known as the Old Boys' School, comprised a master's house and a school house. On one corner of the house section there was an open bell tower with a slated spire rising to a height of 50 feet. Alterations were made to the building in later years and the bell tower and spire were taken down. The school held 100 children, but in 1872 there were only 56 pupils. Of course, with the British School opposite, which was built to take 150 children, it was unlikely that both schools would be full when the adult population was only about 1,300. The two schools amalgamated in 1884 and came under the local school board in 1885. The girls' and infants' departments occupied the old British School, which was enlarged in 1888 to take 190 children. By 1911 100 girls were being taught in one room. The old National School was rebuilt in 1897 for 126 boys. With Upminster's population increasing fast both schools were becoming severely overcrowded and in 1927 a temporary school for 150 infants was opened in St Mary's Lane, followed by the permanent structure in 1928, when all the children were transferred from the British School, although the National School was still used in the 1940s, when the St Mary's Lane School was bomb-damaged. The British School was sited where Barclay's Bank now is and was pulled down in 1936 when the bank and shops were built.

The development of the rest of Station Road, from the Congregational Church on the west side and Talbot's Garage on the east, to the Station all came about in the 20th century and there were no more buildings in Hall Lane until Upminster Hall itself, now the Upminster Golf Club clubhouse.

Although there have been buildings on this site for hundreds of years it is possible that the present building dates back to the 16th century, but it is fairly certain that the staircase and gallery is dated about 1625/50. The property has been added to on many occasions, principally in the 18th century when a northwest wing was added. The medieval stone chapel, dating back to the time when there was an Abbot in residence, was still standing in 1720 and contained a font later given to the parish church, where it is still in use. The chapel was pulled down soon after the donation of the font. It is fairly certain that adjoining the house was a cemetery as skeletons have been found from time to time. The Tithe Barn, now the Agricultural and Folk Museum, was, of course, part of the Manor estate. The thatched timber-framed barn of nine bays was built between 1450 and 1550, but there is no evidence it was ever used for the collection of tithes. The only known tithe barn in Upminster was one adjacent to the Rectory in St Mary's Lane, as the Rector was the only person in the parish collecting tithes.

The boundaries of the Manor have changed through the years, but in the Middle Ages there was a monastic survey which deliniated them -

"First at Tigelhyrste, south towards Marcdike from that dike west to Ingleburn and from that burn north to Beccengare; and from Beccengare north along Wald Street to Stangare; from Stangare north into Mannes land; from Mannesland again to Tigelhyrste..." Years later when Dr Dereham was Rector of St Laurence (1689-1735), he made the following observations on these boundaries which even in the 17th century were difficult to define. Dr Dereham's translation is hard to relate to 20th century landmarks. He said that the northern limit of the manor was Tileshurst, which means a wood incorporating earth suitable for tile making. This wood, he said, was near to Mr Branfil's (Upminster Manor) "above the medicinal spring" and, presumably, he is referring to the old brick and tile works in Bird Lane, not far from the manor house: where the medicinal spring is we do not know. The next reference was to Marcdike and Dr Dereham felt this referred to the boundary with Cranham parish, which was probably marked by a medieval ditch. Turning westward, the next boundary marker is the river Ingrebourne and, after that, Beccengare, which Dr Dereham thought referred to a beacon on a high point, possibly where the Windmill is today. From there going north to Weald Street and Brook Street it is surprising that the boundary was as far north, for usually Upminster Common or a little beyond is thought to be the most northerly boundary of the manor. From this point the line came back southward to near Bird Lane and back to the manor house.

When Ralph Latham was Lord of the Manor in Henry VIII's reign a document named a number of the woods and copses on the estate as Anfedown, Milredon, Newfield, Sallethills, Thickehope and Abbots Common Wood. In 1703, when an indenture was drawn up for a new lease of one of the farms on the estate, some of the fields were named again. This time, some 150 years later, the names are not so much of a mouthful: the fields were Culversfield, Barnefield, Penshott, Crabbeshott, Ley-land, Cowdownes, River Meadows and Grovefield. To the north of the manor house, in what is now the Hall Lane Playing Fields, were four rows of walnut and chestnut trees, which now divide the football field from the hockey pitch. The walnut trees on the two outside lines have long since disappeared, but the chestnuts remain. Standing between the remaining two rows, it can be seen that they lead directly to the house and very possibly the trees were planted with a view to having a carriageway entrance to the manor from the Avon Road end of the estate, although there is no evidence on any maps that there was any entrance in this direction. The maps of the estate show a number of ponds at the rear of the house and it is possible that the symmetrical nature of the pond immediately behind the present club house indicates that it was part of a moat existing a couple of hundred years ago.

Northwards up Hall Lane at its junction with Bird
Lane is Chapmans or Potkiln Farm, which is about two
hundred years old. It has little memorable history of its
own and it is better known for sitting in the centre of
the Upminster brickfields, which were on either side of
Bird Lane immediately behind the farmhouse. This was
occupied by the Knight family in the latter part of the
18th century and Elizabeth Knight was Upminster's only
woman Overseer of the Poor, a post she held between
1798 and 1800, when David Knight was Parish Surveyor for
the north end of Upminster. A subsequent owner of the
property was David Pinchon who owned the windmill on
Upminster Common. This must not be confused with
Tyler's Common, which is on the east of Nag's Head
Lane, whereas Upminster Common was on the west.
    Opposite Chapmans was Martins Farm. It appears
that originally there were three small farms on this side
of Hall Lane; Martins, Motts and Archers. In 1569 Martins
and Motts were held by John Willett. In the 18th century
some of the owners were Messrs Calcot, Carew, Bryan
and Ickling. In the 19th century the farm was owned at
various times by Stephens, Archer, Yeldham, Adcock,
Banking and King. In 1821 Champion Branfil purchased the
110 acres and it then became part of the Upminster Hall
estate. The farmhouse has long since been pulled down,
but some of the farm buildings are still standing as
stables opposite Bird Lane.
    Over the Southend Road (A127) the road starts to
climb slowly towards the commons, but, before arriving,
on the right hand side is Great House, hidden in the trees
about a quarter of a mile before the junction with Nag's
Head Lane. Great House must have been a place of some
renown, for it is mentioned by name on the Chapman &
Andre map of Essex of 1777. Only half a dozen Upminster
properties are on this map, including Great House, some
indication of its importance in the village at the end of
the 18th century. The present house was built in 1802
and, as there are no records of its predecessor, it is
likely that in view of its prominence on the 1777 map,
the former house was much larger. Wilson in his *History*
said that a small stream passed through the property on
its way to the River Ingrebourne and it looked as if it
had been dammed for boating use, forming a lake of

some size. The owner of the house for many years was Lady Clarke Hall, who died at the age of 100 on 16th November, 1979. Her obituary in the *Daily Telegraph* read

"Lady Clarke Hall who has died aged 100 was a notable artist and draughtsman who entered the Slade School of Art in 1894 where her contemporaries included Augustus John and his sister Gwen John, Ambrose McEvoy and William Orpen. Even among such talent she was an outstanding pupil.

"In 1898 she married Sir William Clarke Hall, a barrister and magistrate and went to live in a farmhouse at Upminster where she remained for the next 80 years. Her husband died in 1932. A daughter of the Rev B Waugh, founder of the National Society for the Prevention of Cruelty to Children, she was a remarkable beauty in her student days.

"She continued her artistic career until 1947 and examples of her work can be seen at the Tate Gallery, Victoria and Albert and British Museums, the Fitzwilliam, Cambridge and Manchester City Art Gallery.

"In 1971 a retrospective exhibition of her work was held in London covering her 50 year career and including her early portraits of famous fellow students. She also published two books of poetry."

The small chapel opposite Great House was built in 1850 as a Congregational Chapel on land presented by Mrs Pinchon of Chapmans/Pot Kiln farm. This was the only chapel in the north of the parish and was used quite extensively by the villagers living around the two commons.

Also opposite Great House is Pages Farm, approached from Shepherds Hill, but still within the parish of Upminster. The farmhouse was built in 1663, evidenced by the date carved on a corbel supporting a large oak beam on the ground floor. In the 17th century the farm had 150 acres. Although extensively altered over the centuries there is still evidence of smoke-blackened rafters in the central section of the roof. One of the first recorded owners was Thomas Page at the commencement of the 18th century, who, like Elizabeth Knight of Chapmans, was an Overseer of the Poor. Subsequently the farm was in the ownership of the Holden family, who were rectors of Upminster for many years.

Moving into Nag's Head Lane, having passed the present common on the right, there is still about half a mile of Upminster before the Brentwood boundary is reached.

Brick House farm was off to the right in this stretch: in 1596 it belonged to Walter de Grey and it was in the ownership of the Clothworkers' Company of London in the 18th and 19th centuries. The farm was the site of the first brickworks in Upminster and the excavation of clay was considerable. In the 1850s the crumbling kiln could still be seen although the works had long gone. The farm was partly in the parish of Great Warley, 46 acres being in Upminster.

Back on Tyler's Common there is sited at the far northeast corner Tyler's Hall farm. The name Tylers is supposed to derive from Tigelhurst, which comprise the Saxon words meaning wood and earth fit for tile-making. The wood on the common has disappeared, but brick earth abounds in the area. Tylers Hall farm was enclosed from the common many years ago and, at the time of the Chapman & Andre map of 1777, it was the residence of Capt. John Redman and his wife, Mary, who was the daughter of Andrew Branfil of Upminster Hall.

Upminster Common, on the other side of Nag's Head Lane, where Ivy Lodge Farm is located today, was once called Gaynes Common because of its ownership by that manor. Upminster's other windmill stood on high ground on this common and lasted well into the 19th century.

Down in the valley behind Upminster Common towards the railway line was Goodhouse. During the reign of Henry IV (1399-1413) it was the property of the Deyncourt family and in 1600 the farm was owned by the Lathams. In 1725 the South Sea Company owned the freehold. The farm was immediately adjacent to where the Liverpool Street railway is today and it is noted that when the Eastern Counties Railway Company was building this section in 1840 a labourer by the name of Henry Lock died when the earth gave way.

The remaining building of consequence in the northern part of the village is Great Tomkyns in Tomkyns Lane (formerly Bird Lane). This property, earlier called Great Readings, goes back to the 15th century and mention is made of the house in Pevsner's *Buildings of England*. The property is described as a 15th century yeoman's house with exposed timber framing. The hall goes up the whole height of the building with the east and west wings being two storeyed. There is also a 17th century weatherboarded barn to the south of the house, the whole being contained within a partly-dry moat. Great Tomkyns was all part of the Upminster Hall estate and, after Andrew Branfil bought the manor in 1686, the property was occupied by his daughter, Elizabeth, and her husband, Harman Browse, who was a London merchant. All the occupiers of the property can be traced from the 17th century to when it was sold out of the estate by referring to the Upminster Manor Court Rolls held in the Essex Record Office and available for inspection. The copyhold was purchased from the estate in 1908 by A B Purvis for £300.

Returning to the main crossroads at the 'Bell'. The inn land extended to the gateway in Corbets Tey Road, where there is an entrance to the Upminster Junior School. Before the building of the school among the 20th century development this opening was a walkway from New Place in St Mary's Lane, along a shrubbery beside the Lane that turned behind the 'Bell'. As this gateway is opposite an entrance to the church this was obviously a private walkway from New Place to St Laurence Church.

The next property in Corbets Tey Road was High House with a frontage of 100 yards, standing nearly opposite the church, where Byron Parade is now. High House was built about 1580, although altered much before finally being demolished in 1935 to make way for the shops. The house was a gabled three-storey building with three bedrooms suitable for servants on the top floor and, under that, four more bedrooms and a toilet. On the ground floor was a large entrance hall, a dining room and a drawing room, both 20 feet long, together with a kitchen. Adjacent to the house was a library with an approach covered with trellis work, together with the usual stables and outbuildings associated with large country houses. The gardens ran along Corbets Tey Road and, behind the house, there was a four acre meadow, which became the playing fields for the school. High House was one of the main non-manor houses of the

The Bell, with one of James Matthews' coal wagons.
In the background, the spire of the National School.

Post Office Cottages: W Snelling's shop

village and various noted people lived there from time to time. Dr Dereham, the noted scientist and Rector of St Laurence, lived there about 1700 when the Rectory had fallen into disrepair. A Major Howard, who was killed at Waterloo, resided at this house and he had as an occasional visitor Lord Byron, after whom the parade of shops is named. Another notable resident was Dr William Tabrum, who died in 1869 after having had his coffin made out of one of the branches of the large cedar tree in the front garden. Sir Charles Reilly was one of the last occupiers of High House: in 1906 he designed Upminster Court – now a residence for the elderly opposite Hall Lane Playing Fields.

Adjacent to High House were two rows of cottages, the first well set back from the road with long front gardens. There were seven tenements in the terrace and next to them were ten further cottages, extending as far as Woolworths is today. The first set was built in the early part of the 19th century, while the ten were constructed a little earlier, in 1780. This second row was built much closer to the road, with short front gardens, but very long at the back. The cottage at either end was slightly different, standing a little forward of the others and being slightly larger with a high roof. These end properties were described as large, well-built tenements, with two bedrooms and two attic rooms – which account for the high roofs. On the ground floor of one was a shop and a kitchen, with a cellar below, and out the back there was a building described as a cart lodge or slaughterhouse. The shop was run by two generations of the Allen family between 1790 and 1828; firstly by John Allen, and then his daughter, Jane. The shop was a general store that subsequently became the village Post Office and the row of cottages became known as Post Office Cottages. Later Miss Emma Lee became Postmistress, this very respected lady being the daughter of Robert Lee, the Vestry Clerk in the mid-19th century. She retired in 1895 and died three years later. Both rows of cottages remained until 1937, when they were pulled down for the shopping development.

Opposite the cottages there were no buildings at all, as these fields were glebe lands belonging to the church.

On the east side the next house was West Lodge, which is still standing, being approached by a narrow drive between the shops. In the Ordnance Survey map for 1868 it is referred to as Bow Villa. The house has changed a great deal since Sir James Esdaile had the property built in 1785 on the site of a former house. The first tenant was Samuel Hammond, the contractor. When the Gaynes estate was sold in 1839 Samuel Hammond's son, William, bought the house for £520. It was fairly large, with three principal bedrooms and three more for servants, two parlours, a drawing room and a study, together with the usual kitchen and ancillary buildings which included a dairy and a brewhouse. There was stabling for two horses. The property passed through various hands during the next hundred years, until the frontage to Corbets Tey Road was sold for more shops and flats in 1938. Before the ground at the rear was turned into a car park for the banqueting rooms and the premises extended, there was a grass tennis court and a very pleasant garden.

The next property along Corbets Tey Road was Hunt's farm, which stood opposite Stewart Avenue. This was a tall three-storey square farmhouse and another of Sir James Esdaile's building projects. It appears that there had been various previous farmhouses on the site before the last rebuilding in 1775. A hundred years earlier in 1673 Sir Benjamin Wright of Cranham Hall owned the farm and, late in 1729, Sir Nathan Wright was the owner, there being 30 acres of land. The land to the rear of the farm was called Eastfields and maybe Springfield Gardens should have borne this name, although it is likely there was a spring in the vicinity as well. The Esdaile family were owners of Hunt's until 1839, when it was purchased by William Colls. By this time the farm had grown and its farmland extended from Springfield Gardens to Cranston Park Avenue. Prior to the sale of the farm the tenant was James Nokes of the Windmill, who lived at Hunt's until he died in 1838. Henry Joslin bought the farm in 1890 for £5,200 and his brother, Walter, lived at Hunt's, farming the land. Following the deaths of the Joslins the farm was sold for building development with the farmhouse being demolished in 1937/8. There was a pond at the rear of the farmhouse roughly where the

Hunt's

Hoppy Hall

Baptist Church is sited and if this pond was fed by a spring, then maybe the road has been correctly named after all!

Almost opposite Hunt's, where the Post Office sorting office and the petrol station are sited was Hoppy Hall. Wilson says that a farm on this site was called Gladmans in the 16th century and owned by Ralph Latham, whereas on a manor map of 1752 it is referred to as Mr Groom's land. The farm and land covered all that area along Corbets Tey Road as far as Little Gaynes Lane and probably back as far as the Ingrebourne. In 1774 the property was owned by John Mayor, passing to Sir James Esdaile when he married Mayor's daughter. Prior to the rebuilding of Gaynes manor house Sir James held his Court Baron (manor court) at Hoppy Hall. In 1819 the house was purchased by the Rev. John Clayton and had, at that time, 100 acres. On Mr Clayton's death Henry Joslin senior bought the farm, which was sold to J William Benn in 1891. J William Benn was the father of Lord Stansgate, whose son renounced the title to revert to the familiar Anthony Wedgwood Benn, M.P. There were various owners during the 20th century before the property and farm were sold for housing development in 1935/6. The front garden boasted a very large cedar tree, reared at New Place and transferred when 15 years old and 12 feet high to Hoppy Hall about 1790. Wilson says that when a branch fell in 1852 it was 50 feet long, while whole spread of the tree was some 98 feet across.

After the fields of Hunt's and Hoppy Hall, the next landmark is the junction of Corbets Tey Road and Little Gaynes Lane, which was the start of the land forming part of Gaynes manor. At this point was sited one of two lodges, the other being somewhere near the corner of Little Gaynes Lane and The Grove. Little Gaynes Lane takes its name from a small house called Little Gaynes which was 100 yards or so past the junction with The Grove towards Hacton Lane. In fact, Little Gaynes Lane was previously called Hacton Lane, as it led to Hacton House further down the road. The lodge at Gaynes Cross, as the junction was called, was probably built about 1770 and on the Tithe map of 1843 it was described as two tenements and gardens let to sundry occupiers. The Gaynes Cross corner was also the site of

Gaynes manor pound, where stray animals were placed until claimed by their owners. The other lodge was called West Gate Lodge and was built in 1846 being used as a coachman's lodge. The roof was thatched and this caught fire in 1908. As the nearest fire station was in Billet Lane, Hornchurch, the fire took some time to put out, but the house was rebuilt as before and survived until the 1930s before it was demolished for housing development.

From Domesday until the 20th century there have been many houses on the site of Gaynes manor, but few drawings or descriptions have been preserved. Earlier in this book there was a description of Sir James Esdaile's new Classical manor house and there is a pen portrait of the previous manor house owned by George Montgomery, dated 1752. The house was set well back from the road on the south side of Little Gaynes Lane. It was described as a grange, which is something between and large farm-house and a mansion. There were two high walls about 50/60 yards apart running down either side of the front lawn to Little Gaynes Lane. Along the road joining the two walls was a high spiked iron railing with central gates in Queen Anne style. The drive from these gates to the house was lined with trees. On the north side of Little Gaynes Lane, opposite the house, was an eight acre field called the Image field, containing at its centre a female figure draped in robes.

Following Montgomery's death Sir James Esdaile bought Gaynes in 1770 and began his building and re-building programme referred to in Chapter 2. The stream flowing through the south part of the estate (now Park-lands Open Space) was dammed to form a lake for boating and a small bridge was built at one end and an island formed in the middle, the whole area being surrounded in trees. A pavilion and small water fall were built at the other end. Esdaile's mansion was very largely demolished in 1820 and, in 1821, the Rev. John Clayton built Gaynes Villa a little to the east of the old house. This was much smaller and built in the Tudor Gothic style. Wilson's description, from first-hand knowledge, speaks of an entrance door of bold proportions between butresses on the north front, which shows that, like its predecessors, it faced Little Gaynes Lane. Above the front door was a corbelled window, breaking up the otherwise plain front. On the west side were three mullioned windows, one above the other, in the perpendicular style fitted with stained glass giving light to the staircase and main hall. The main rooms were on the south of the building and had large bay windows looking down the parkland to the lake. Many of the fields around the manor house had names and those between Little Gaynes Lane and the lake were called Frogwell Mead, Golden Mead, Pennybrooks, Great Shillings and Little Shillings, Great Barking Field and Little Barking Field, together with Twelve Acres piece and Seven Acre piece. The new Gaynes manor and the other properties and buildings on the estate remained until 1927, when they were all pulled down for residential development.

Further down Little Gaynes Lane at its junction with Hacton Lane is Hactons. Despite its being on the edge of the parish Hactons was one of the principal properties both in terms of size and in respect of its owners. It was built about 1770 by William Braund who lived in the house until he died in 1774. Wilson once again gives a full description of the house in his 1856 book *Sketches of Upminster*. It consisted of a central building with stone quoins at the angles and extensive wings abutting the sides, but not projecting forward. Up a flight of steps to the front door there was a well proportioned portico and above this a Venetian window giving height to the saloon that occupied the whole depth of the house. A bold cornice along the top of the house carried a balustraded parapet and above this a pediment, making the whole front look very effective. When the house was unoccupied during World War II it was found that trespassers were gaining entry through a secret passage leading from the grounds to a small room off the hall which had in it a moveable dresser. Prior to Sir James Esdaile's development of Gaynes and his Upminster estates, Hacton itself boasted many acres of parkland behind the house. When Sir Thomas Lennard was the owner in 1800 he was a Captain in the Volunteer Cavalry of the district and reviewed his troops at Hactons. A former Hacton House stood just outside the parish boundary across the River Ingrebourne at Hacton Bridge. The house was approached just over the bridge on the left (going from Upminster) by a gateway that was the drive ascending to elevated ground overlooking the Ingrebourne valley. The house was a long, red-brick building of two storeys containing nine windows and having a portico reaching to the top of the building. The house was pulled down in 1790. The drive to the house was flanked by an avenue of oriental plane trees still standing 70 years after the house was pulled down. In the 1850s Wilson noted that there was another building in the grounds of the old house which was last used as a brick barn and which could well have been the original mansion. Wilson put the date of this former building at about 1450/1500 by dating the fireplace still existing in the brick barn.

William Braund, who built the 'new' Hactons, was probably much wealthier than his Lord of the Manor, Sir James Esdaile, as it was commonplace for London merchants to have more wealth than the large landowners. Lords of the Manor tended to over-rule their tenants in times of dispute until, of course, one came up against someone like William Braund, who was prepared to stand up for himself and support the rights of other tenants. In 1773 Braund enclosed a piece of land in front of Hactons, near the road, with posts and rails. Through his steward Sir James ordered that the fence be taken down, despite Braund's explanation that it was to stop people falling into the ditch at night. The fence was duly taken down, but later Sir James himself fenced off an area in St Mary's Lane, opposite the Junior School, where there was a watering place for the villagers and which was their right. William Braund took the gate off its hinges and left it on the ground after watering his horse. Anyone who wished to get to the water did so despite the gate being put back and eventually Sir James backed down. William Braund was later allowed to put his fence back in front of Hactons. During the 1939/45 War the army was billetted at Hactons and thereafter the property was considerably altered and converted into flats.

Hacton was a hamlet within the parish of Upminster and, in the 18th century, there were many cottages sprawling along Hacton Lane from the bridge over the Ingrebourne to the White Hart tavern and round the corner to Park Corner Farm. In 1854 this hamlet, as well as that of Corbets Tey, suffered from a serious epidemic of cholera: in all 100 cases of diarrhoea and cholera were diagnosed, of which three were fatal, with all the cases coming from residences within the two hamlets. The cause was the stagnant water and absence of proper drainage.

Park Corner farm is in Park Farm Road, which lies between Hacton Lane and Harwood Hall Lane. In the 18th century the farm had only 66 acres, but under the owner- ship of Richard Bright of Orsett the farm grew to 140 acres in the mid 1800s.

Back in Corbets Tey Road, going towards Corbets Tey, the next property is Tadlows (251 Corbets Tey Road), still standing. It is unknown when the first house was built here, but it goes back before the Esdaile building period, as it is mentioned in 1704, when it was called Rolfs. At this time it was held by Mrs Susannah Latham and had 40 acres of fields. Later, in 1720, it was called Peacocks and four acres of land were referred to as Peacock Grove. Sir James Esdaile bought the house and land from John Mayor when it contained 60 acres, but when later bought by James Nokes there were a mere 20 acres. Wilson says that Sir James Esdaile built the present house when the land was in his possession. The property is on three floors, having six bedrooms, two living rooms and two kitchens. On the Ordnance Survey map of 1868 there is shown on the south side of the garden in a small paddock a pond with a well, which is where Tadlows Close is now.

Still going towards Corbets Tey, at the foot of the hill on the left hand side was Foxhall. The house was just on the Upminster side of the little stream that crosses under the road into the Gaynes manor lake. The house was built in 1718 and was originally called Osbournes. In 1765 it bore the name Fox Hunters Hall, but later occupants changed it the name to simply Foxhall. The house was a solid square building with small wings either side. The south wing formed an elegant drawing room. There was a lofty flight of steps leading to the front door, which was highly ornamented incorpor- ating a cherub's head. The roof was very highly pitched with large flat chimney shafts, the whole having the look of a French style mansion. The Osborne family was in possession in 1600, as evidenced by a list of jurors at a Court Baron of Gaynes manor when William Latham was

London's

Corbets Tey, Upminster.

Corbets Tey village: the Huntsman & Hounds, High House and
Bearblock Cottages on the left: the smithy on the right

Lord of the Manor. One noteable occupier about 1800 was General Poyntz, who was Silver Stick to George III. The Poyntz family has a very long history mainly connected with the Gloucestershire area, but in North Ockendon church there are various monuments to the family. They owned land in Upminster and North Ockendon parishes and, in 1601, Gabriel Poyntz was Chairman of the Jurors at the Court Baron of Gaynes manor. Foxhall Road has now been built on the site of the house and its grounds, which had diminished to only 30 acres by the 1930s, although in earlier times the property had more than double this.

Just before Corbets Tey village there was one further property of consequence - Londons, which stood where Londons Close is now, on the opposite side to Foxhall and halfway up the hill. This tall, square Georgian farmhouse was built by Sir James Esdaile in about 1790 and took its name from Doctor London who lived there and was the parish doctor. This 54 acre farm was purchased by Samuel Hammond from the Gaynes estate in 1820. Subsequently H A Gilliat bought the farm in 1876 bringing it back to Gaynes. A photograph of the house taken in about 1910 shows it to be a fairly solid three-storey building with a large square front porch. Wilson writes that in about 1850 the then owner, Thomas Price, enlarged the house and enclosed it with a handsome iron railing, which is still in the 1910 photograph.

At the top of the hill is Corbets Tey village and it is surprising to note how little it has changed over the past hundred years. According to the historian, Morant, Corbets Tey derives its name from an ancient owner of the area, together with the Saxon word meaning enclosure - Corbet's enclosure. A more popular, but less likely, explanation is the one concerning Queen Elizabeth I on her way to Tilbury to review her fleet which was threatened by the Spanish Armada. It is said that she passed through the village and, on admiring the scenery, called to one of her aides, "Corbet stay!" There was a Corbet family close to the throne at this time, which makes the story feasible, but Morant's explanation is the more credible.

The 'Huntsman and Hounds' public house has been on the same site for 200 years, although the present building was only erected in 1896. Adjacent to the pub is High House, dating back 300 years. Opposite is the Old Cottage, which was once an inn called the Royal George in 1789, subsequently becoming the George. In a directory of 1835 the inn had become the George and Dragon. The house is thought to be about 400 years old. As an inn it finally closed its doors in 1901, when the owners Ind, Coope & Co., Ltd., transferred the licence to Romford. At one time there was adjacent to the cottages – it was originally more than a single dwelling – a smithy and many older Upminster residents can, I am sure, remember watching horses being shod until the late 1940s.

Back across the road it is noted that the previous inn was called the Huntsmen and Hounds; the name seems to have changed after the rebuilding and maybe is just a signwriter's error. There is no record of how long an inn has stood on the site, but it probably dates back to the early 18th century, as the licensee in 1769 was Hill Bromfield. Joseph Lee, who later took over the 'Bell' was also at one time landlord in Corbets Tey. With the hamlet's population being so small it is surprising that it could support more than one inn, although it is probable that the publicans had other interests and did not rely solely on income from the public house.

High House dates from about 1700, although the wings date much earlier. With its commanding view at the top of the hill and built before Londons, the house looked directly towards the land of Gaynes manor as, of course, when built the parkland of Gaynes and the lake had not been laid out. When the lake was formed, with its orna- mental brick bridge, there was a turf road leading from the bridge to an octagonal cottage on the corner of Harwood Hall Lane and opposite High House. The cottage was built as a lodge for Gaynes, sited on the southeast corner of the estate. As there was this lodge it is probable that the turf road was used as an entrance to the manor house for people approaching from the Corbets Tey direction.

High House had various owners over the years including Doctor London – before he moved to Londons – and Mrs Poyntz – widow of the General, who earlier lived at Foxhall. In 1804 High House was a boarding school run by Mr Saunders, who was exempt from military service during the Napoleonic Wars due to lameness in one arm. Unfortunately Mr Saunders went bankrupt and the property was put up for auction in 1830. Since then there have been many owners, but it is good to see that the small farm of about 30 acres is still used as a small-holding, producing fruit and vegetables for local consumption.

The first cottage in Harwood Hall Lane was also an inn, known as the 'Anchor'; it ceased to trade in 1896. Next to the 'Anchor', or the Old Cottage, as it now is, are Bearblock Cottages, which probably take their name from John Bearblock of Hornchurch Hall in 1856.

Two other buildings in Corbets Tey village are worth noting: the first was Keelings, adjacent to what is now the 'Huntsman and Hounds' car park, at Cabbage Corner. The property was a typical Essex weatherboard cottage standing sideways to the road and not to be confused with Keelings Cottages, which were round the corner on the other side of the road. These were probably named after Joseph Keeling, who was the parish surveyor for the highways covering the south of the parish in 1766. It is a possibility that part of Keelings was also an inn and Wilson, in describing the cottage, thought that from the construction of the roof and rafters the building dated from the time of Henry VII or VIII. Maybe this was the inn where Elizabeth stayed overnight on her way to Tilbury.

Branching from Ockendon Road is Sunnings Lane, wherein stand two of the oldest houses in the parish. First is Great Sunnings, lying well back off the road on the east side, while Little Sunnings is on the other side of the road a little further on. Externally Great Sunnings has been changed much over the years, but inside there is evidence that the panelling dates from the latter part of Elizabeth I's reign and the house could have been built before 1600. There must have been a previous property on the site, for in the reign of Henry VII (1485-1509) Great Sunnings paid to the King a fee of three wolves annually while, as a comparison, Stubbers in North Ockendon paid two wolves: this fee was one of the ways that the King had of exterminating wolves from the countryside. In 1673 Great Sunnings was owned by Sir Benjamin Wright of Cranham Hall and later by the Russell family that owned

Stubbers. Unfortunately, much of the interior, including the panelling and Adam fireplace, was sold and sent to the United States during this century.

Although less is known of Little Sunnings, it is believed to be even older than Great Sunnings. Previously the farmhouse was called Old Sunnings and, before that, Old Sullens. On Chapman & Andre's map of 1777 both the Sunnings houses are spelt as now and consequently these other names for Little Sunnings must date back before the 18th century. Incidentally, this map of Essex made one of its few mistakes by placing Great Sunnings on the corner of the Ockendon Road where the Crematorium is today. We know little of the owners of Little Sunnings despite its great age, although in 1692 Philip Masham willed the farm to the Feltmakers' Company together with 40 acres. The conditions were that the Company distribute every Christmas to twenty poor hatmakers 20 shillings a piece and also £5 per annum to Katherine Parsons, a spinster relation of Masham, during her lifetime. The Feltmakers' Company did not run the farm, but there were various tenants during the time of their ownership. Little Sunnings is still a farm today.

Sunnings Lane was once more important than it is today, as Wilson in the 1850s refers to it as the footway to Stifford, while travelling that way today would be through North Ockendon using the road past the Crematorium. On the 1872 Ordnance Survey map the road turns sharply to the right out of the village by Keelings directly into Sunnings Lane, as if this was the normal line of the road. Both routes meet in South Ockendon village and the Sunnings Lane route is a little shorter than today's main road.

Turning right at the top of Corbets Tey Hill takes one to Harwood Hall to the south of the lane bearing its name. The present house was built by Sir James Esdaile in 1782 for his son-in-law, George Stubbs, but there was a house on the site well before this, for it can be seen that in 1704 the property was owned by Mrs Mary Doe. George Stubbs married Sir James' daughter, Mary, and they lived at Harwood Hall until Sir Thomas Lennard became the occupant in 1801, having previously lived at Hactons and subsequently moving to Belhus, the family seat at Aveley, in 1804. Captain P Z Cox bought the house from the Gaynes estate, as he did Foxhall, living there until his death in 1858, when he left Harwood Hall, High House and Foxhall to A Z Button. Many of the occupants of the Upminster country houses were tenants, like Sir Thomas Lennard, and also Colonel Henry Holmes, who later built and lived in Grey Towers, Hornchurch. Wilson described the property in 1856 as being called Harewood and having 74 acres. By 1881 the estate had fallen to 21 acres. The house itself was enlarged about 1840 and castellated in 1881, since when it has changed very little, retaining its pleasant atmosphere of a fine country house with lawns and shrubberies, benefitting by being somewhat set back from the road.

The remaining section of this southern part of Upminster is the tract of farmland between Sunnings Lane, on the east, and the Aveley Road, on the west. Aveley Road formed the western parish boundary, following the road down to the little stream that comes from Running Water Wood. Separating this area east to west is Bramble Lane, to the north of which was Chafford Heath. The heath itself has been absorbed into the farms in the district, although Wilson wrote that there used to be an ancient house on the heath 300 years old, but in ruins when he wrote in 1856. Bush Farm, north of the heath, dated back to at least 1694, some of the carpentry being earlier. In that year the farm was owned by Abraham Tavener, who also held Chafford Heath. From then it passed to Thomas Roberts in 1704 and, at the end of the century, the owner was the ubiquitous Sir James Esdaile. In 1809 John Russell became the owner and thenceafter Champion Russell. In the mid-19th century the farm owned 140 acres. The site of Bush farm is approached by the private road off the Aveley Road, where the large gravel pits are located on the left hand side after passing Gerpins Lane, travelling south.

Close by is Bramble Farm in Bramble Lane, dating back about 200 years. The owner in 1846 was Thomas Circuit, a market gardener who had a similar business nearer London. The farm had 56 acres during his owner-ship and he built two double cottages considered at the time to be of very good design.

On the southern boundary is the farm called Cockhides which, although in Upminster, formed part of

Sir Thomas Lennard's Belhus estate in Aveley. In addition to Cockhides Farm, which had 47 acres, there were many other acres of farm and woodland in the southern tip of Upminster in the Belhus estate. The survey of 1842 records Sir Thomas and other members of his family owning in all 185 acres in this part of Upminster.

Returning to the 'Bell' crossroads, the road to the east is St Mary's Lane, known as Cranham Road until 1922. The parish was narrow at its centre and the boundary with Cranham parish is where Argyle Gardens joins St Mary's Lane. On the south of this road there was only one property – New Place, whose estate extended from the 'Bell' Inn to Argyle Gardens and back as far as Sunnyside Gardens. New Place was a manor house with no manorial rights and there had been a building on the site for many centuries. The last building was that erected by Sir James Esdaile in 1775, when he occupied the house after his marriage to the daughter of John Mayor of Hoppy Hall. Previously it had been in the possession of the Latham family back as far as 1550 and Ralph Latham lived there after he parted with the manors of Gaynes and Upminster Hall in 1640. The Esdaile family kept control until 1839 when it passed through various owners until finally being demolished in 1924. The stable block remains and still stands today.

The house itself was on the 'Bell' side of the stable block and coach house. The house was built of red brick, the same as the stables, quadrangular and winged. It was a large house with 12 bedrooms and the western wing formed a large drawing room 35 feet long, 25 feet wide and 15 feet high. The eastern end was the servants' quarters. The centre was elevated with a pillared porch supporting an ornamental bay window. The large drawing room had many mirrors which obviously made the room look even larger. Sir James Esdaile built the room in this style as he was very fond of dancing and used the room for balls, there being no public place for miles around of this size.

The stable block, known to us now as The Clock-house, was surmounted by a turret clock that became known in the village in the 19th century as the 'great' or 'village' clock. Part of the gardens and the ornamental moat have been retained as a public garden.

On the north side of St Mary's Lane there have been, for the past two hundred years, a row of cottages extending from the Cosy Corner, opposite the 'Bell' all the way to the 'Mason's Arms' where the parish boundary lies. Wilson refers to various cottages in this stretch of road, naming Grove Cottage, Oak Cottage, Oak Place, and Field Cottage as the main residence. Oak Cottage was built for the Rev J Jubb, who was curate of St Laurence from 1737 to 1763. The cottages along this stretch were continuous until that part opposite Tudor Gardens, where there was a small field where Sir James Esdaile grew hops.

The 'Mason's Arms' at the parish boundary was rebuilt in 1928, the previous inn having been there for about a hundred years. The majority of the properties, including the 'Mason's', were part of the Upminster Hall estate, although the Lord of the Manor had no rights over the properties, as they were all copyhold. This equates with a very long lease in modern parlance and usually copyholders bought out their copyhold for a small sum, thus making the title freehold.

The Mason's Arms, about 1910

ST LAURENCE CHURCH and its RECTORS

It is quite likely that a Saxon church stood in the elevated centre of Upminster for many years prior to the Norman Conquest. The fact that it is not sited near either of the two principal manor houses, which was usually the case, suggests that it may have served a much wider area a thousand years ago. The earliest known Essex church is at Bradwell-on-Sea where, in about 650, Cedd, the brother of St Chad, arrived to preach and build St Peter's. It is quite likely that many churches sprang up in Essex about that time: St Chad's travels in the area are marked by place names like Chadwell Heath, Chadwell St Mary and Chafford [Chad's ford] and it is reasonable to assume that he paid a visit to Upminster.

The patronal name St Laurence comes from one of the early Christian martyrs who is believed to have been born in Husea, Spain, in the third century. He became a deacon of Rome at the time of Pope Sixtus I and, during the persecution of that time, he was called upon to deliver up the treasures of the church; he produced the poor and sick of the city who were in his care. His refusal to hand over valuables resulted in his being broiled on a gridiron over a fire. In 1911 the church erected a weathervane in the shape of a gridiron to honour St Laurence.

The original church would have been built of wood or wattles and mud and set in a clearing, for most of Essex in the 7th century was well wooded with Epping Forest, for example, stretching from east London to the Suffolk borders.

The next church on the site dated from the time of John (1199-1216), evidenced by parts of the tower. The church then would have been built of stone with great wooden arches. The first reference to the church was a grant made in 1223 by Viel Engaine, Lord of Gaynes

Manor, in the sum of 40 shillings a year from Upminster church to the Priory of Worspring, Somerset. The Manor of Gaynes owned the right to appoint rectors of the church and this advowson, as it is called, passed through various hands until it was bought by William Holden of Birmingham in 1780. The living remained with the family until the 1970s.

After the rebuilding of the church in about 1200, Sir John Engayne had the Engayne Chapel on the north side of the church constructed between 1270 and 1290 as a burial place for the family. In the 17th century the chapel was rebuilt by Hamlett Clarke and again, in 1771, Sir James Esdaile had a hand in changing the chapel by excavating a family vault below. In 1839, when he sold New Place, Sir James also sold the rights he had of the chapel. Later tenants of New Place rented the pews in the chapel to other families.

A finely carved open oak screen was provided for the chapel in the 15th century, but at the time of the rebuilding in 1861-2, it was thrown out and lay in a ditch for a year, before being rescued, renovated and put back into the church. In 1638 the church and spire were struck by lightning and caught fire. Fortunately the bells had been taken down at the time and were not damaged. A new pulpit was installed in 1740 and the church still retains the 15th century font from the chapel of Upminster Hall.

In 1776 Charles Hornby, who lived at Foxhall, left £200 in his will so that a gallery could be built for the psalm singers of Upminster parish church. His brother, William, would not hand over the money and the Church Vestry employed a solicitor to compel William to fulfil the terms of the will. Incidentally, the solicitor was George Stubbs, son-in-law of James Esdaile. The money was eventually ceded in 1782 and a gallery was built of mahogany, with elaborate carvings. This gallery was re-placed by a lower and larger version in 1845, but this was dispensed with when the major rebuilding took place in 1861/2.

The rebuilding, in stone, was accomplished partly from a gift from the younger J R Holden, the church being rebuilt to the design of W G Bartlett. The seating was greatly increased, but this entailed the removal of all the old fittings many of which were of Elizabethan origin. In 1906 the vestry was built and repair work was undertaken to the tower and the spire. Choir stalls were inserted in 1906 and the church was lit for the first time by gas in 1912. A new Lady Chapel was erected beyond the Gaynes Chapel in 1928/9 with the chancel being taken into the nave and a new one built. A south chapel of St George was also added at this time. Finally, new vestries were built east of the south chapel in 1937.

There were four bells in 1552 - and there are still four today. Number One Bell is dated about 1480 and bears the inscription "Sancte Gabriele ora pro nobis", a reminder of the days when bells were given names, were solemnly baptised and even had sponsors. Number Two Bell is dated 1974: one of its predecessors was recast in 1602 and subsequently sold in 1823. Number Three is dated 1583 and was cast by Robert Mot of Whitechapel, the inscription reading "Robert Mot made me 1583". Number Four was recast in 1602 and is inscribed "God save our noble Queen Elizabeth 1602 RH". In 1818 Number Two was badly cracked following the fall of a beam during repairs to the tower: it was not replaced for over a hundred and fifty years.

Most of the stained glass windows are of 20th century origin, with the exception of that in the north aisle, dated 1630. The armorial bearings in this window are those of the families Stanley, Engayne, Deyncourt and Latham. The 20th century east window depicts St Cedd carrying a model of the first church and St Laurence holding a model of the church as it was in 1930. The east window of St George's Chapel depicts the three Essex saints Helena, Mellitus and Ethelburga and replaces a window damaged by bomb blast in 1940.

The church holds only three items of plate of any consequence. A silver chalice, dated 1608, inscribed "The Communion Cupp of Upmynster" is the only example of Jacobean plate in the Deanery. This chalice weighs just over 12 ounces and is $9\frac{1}{2}$ inches high and $3\frac{1}{2}$ inches in diameter. There is also a silver paten, dated 1704, and a silver alms dish, 9 inches in diameter, dated 1686 and inscribed "Upminster" on the reverse. In 1586 the church was broken into and possibly the Elizabethan communion cup was stolen then, as the new vessel was inscribed so that it would be easily recognisable in the future.

Brass rubbing has increased in popularity in recent years and, despite pilferage in many churches, Upminster is fortunate in having eight historic brasses. The oldest is dated about 1455 and is of Elizabeth Deyncourt. There is another of Nicholas Wayte, Lord of Gaynes manor, and of Ellen, his wife, dated 1545. A third is of Gerardt D'Ewes in full armour dated 1591. It appears that all these brasses were once part of larger and older works of art. On their reverses are fragments of figures of abbots and parts of inscriptions: brasses of this type are called palimpsests. The others are not recognisable, but do contain one of a civilian dated 1540. There are many monuments around the church walls and, if one spends a little time wandering around, many monuments can be seen of the principal Upminster families to the present.

The village church was invariably one of the wealthiest places in the locality, not just for the plate in its possession, but for the land and cattle it owned. During the religious upheaval of the 16th and 17th centuries Henry VIII split the English church from Rome, but he retained the same church service, despite a movement in the nation to do away with all reminders of Catholicism. After Henry's death in 1547 his son, Edward VI, made the complete change to Protestantism, destroying all relics of the old Catholic church. As there was no more use for various items which the church had previously used for Mass, these were sold off by the clergy privately and, to stop this, an inventory was ordered by the Crown of all possessions of each church. That for Upminster is recorded as -

Two chalices in gilt, one weighing $16\frac{1}{2}$ ounces and the other 11 ounces; three copes, one purple velvet grounded with gold, one green velvet, one red silk; four vestments, two of red velvet and two of silk; three albs; a cross cloth of red silk; two towels and a diaper towel; two streams of green silk; eleven altar cloths; two stoles of red velvet; two pewter candlesticks; two pewter basins; two surplices for the priest; the three church bells and three small hand bells. The date of the inventory was 3rd October, 1552.

The sheep and cattle owned by the church were often hired out to villagers, the funds they produced going to the upkeep of the church. The inventory records who was in possession of church livestock. Apparently, prior to the inventory the clergy had sold a red velvet vestment to Ralph Latham and it is recorded that this garment was in the hands of Ralph Latham's wife, who liked it so much that she declined to hand it back. Amongst others who had purchased or leased church property there is mentioned a Guild of Trinity, a medieval religious guild, that owned two cows.

All these possessions were claimed for the King through three Commissioners, who were William Berners, William Ayloff of Hornchurch, and Anthony Browne of Brentwood (who founded Brentwood School). The Commissioners allowed one chalice to be retained for future use in the church, together with one cope of green and red velvet, three towels, six table cloths and two surplices.

A year after Upminster's inventory Edward died and Mary came to the throne, bringing with her the aim of the restoration of Catholicism. Protestant ministers were removed and it is believed that the rector at that time, Edward Keble, suffered this fate. Only five years later Elizabeth was crowned and her policy was to adopt a compromise between the two faiths. In 1559 the Act of Uniformity was passed ordering that all worship be uniform. The cope was to be worn for sacraments and the surplice for other ministrations. There were many clergy, however, who would not comply with these new rules and they were forced to leave the living, often being replaced with men of little learning. William Washer was appointed Rector in 1558 and referred to in a Puritan list as an ignorant and unpreaching minister. Apparently he was also a grocer and in those days it was unheard of to be both in business and in the church. He was rector until 1609 and during his time had many quarrels with the Latham family, there being various records in the Archdeacons' Courts of his misdeeds. Although the Lathams owned both Upminster Hall and Gaynes manors they did not own the church living as it had been sold elsewhere and consequently the Lathams could not get rid of William Washer. In 1574 there was a row actually in the church when William Latham called Washer a knave. A few years later, in 1587, the church court records that Washer was guilty of not carrying out his duties properly and for letting the church property fall into decay. His own churchwardens reported him for not making repairs to his parsonage and adjoining buildings and also for cutting and spoiling various trees in the churchyard. William Washer was getting old and there are various other reports of disputes with the Lathams over tithes which he probably could not collect, leading inevitably to the deterioration of the church and the parsonage.

Washer was eventually succeeded by John Bowle, William Halke and then, in 1615, by Michael Halke, whose nine year stay was also fraught with problems. His parish-ioners reported him for not carrying out his duties properly in that he would not instruct the young of the parish in the basics of the religion. He was also reported for frequenting taverns, fighting and for not being properly dressed for services. In 1618 he was accused of misconduct with his maid, who bore a child in 1619. During this year he was not attending the church and an assistant curate took the services. By 1620 Halke was suspended altogether, although he still lived at the rectory until 1624, when he was deprived of his living.

Christopher Denne followed Michael Halke, who, incidentally, still drew £40 from the revenue of the church while he was alive, and after Denne came John Halke, who was appointed in 1638. The Civil War broke out in 1642 and four years later the Puritans removed Halke from the living. Halke took his case to the House of Lords, but lost not only Upminster but the right to preach at all. Fortunately for him the Commonwealth ended in 1660 and, with Charles II on the throne, the Puritan rector was removed and John Halke returned to the benefice. In 1662 the Act for the Uniformity of Public Prayer was passed, which, as its name suggests, laid down instructions for using the prayer book and the form of service. You would have thought that John Halke would have welcomed these changes following the problems of the previous years, but he did not agree with the provisions of the Act and resigned the same year.

Upminster now reverted to being a quiet and peaceful village, as far as the church was concerned, and a succession of rectors carried out their duties in accordance with the new Act and all was well with the church and its parishioners.

A further inventory of the church was taken in 1683, giving a far different picture compared to the Catholic splendour of the previous list.

"There is an old linen cloth for the Communion Table. There is a flagon and a silver chalice with a cover to it. There is a bason to give the offerings upon. A Bible which must be new bound and two common prayer books. A very handsome rail before the Communion Table. A Book of Homilys Cannons and Articles and a Table of degrees of Marriage. There is a pulpit cushion. There are four bells in good order. There wants a napkin for the Communion Table, a plate for to administer bread upon, a new naper clothe for the Communion Table. There wants a carpet of green cloth for the Communion Table. The cover of the font wants mending. The pews in the body of the church and the lower end wants to be boarded, especially those on the north side. The Chancel must be made even in ye pavement. The Churchwardens to provide hassocks and place them in the pews of the church for the people to kneel on."

The inventory goes on to say more about what is wrong with the church, concluding with comment on the structure, saying that the St Mary's Chapel, belonging to Sir Thomas Skipwith, was in need of repair and the beams were rotten.

Following John Halke's resignation there were three more rectors over the next 27 years before William Derham was appointed in 1689. William Derham was the most eminent rector Upminster ever had and probably the most well-known for many miles around. Much is known about him through his interest in clockmaking and Charles Aked carried out much research on the famous rector, publishing a number of articles in 1970, on which the following is based.

William Derham was born near Worcester in 1657. Although his parents were poor, he was a clever student and went to Trinity College, Oxford, in 1675. He obtained his Batchelor of Arts degree in 1679 and so impressed the President of the College that he was introduced to the Bishop of Salisbury and thereafter took holy orders, eventually entering the church. Derham's first living was Wargrave in Berkshire, which he took up in 1682, two years later marrying Isabella Darrell of Kingsclere. Derham stayed 7 years at Wargrave, until being presented by Mrs Jane Bray to the living of Upminster on 31st August, 1689. The curate was the Rev Hugh Price, who was appointed three years earlier and who stayed at Upminster for a total of 32 years. William Derham did not live at the rectory, due to its dilapidation, but resided instead at High House, just opposite the church in Corbets Tey Road. The old rectory was not demolished until 30 years after Derham's death and this building stood in part of the gardens of the new rectory that was built in 1765. Derham had moved into a village of about 350 people, including children, and his income was £200 per annum, which was a goodly sum in those days. However, this income had to be collected from the parish-ioners in the form of tithes and this was not always easy, as had been shown by previous incumbents, but William Derham did not have the squabbles that his predecessors had with the important members of the community and consequently had little trouble collecting the tithe.

Rectors in those days had plenty of time on their hands and this gave Derham the opportunity to visit London to meet his friends, who were both intellectual and varied. His interests were natural history, math-ematics, astronomy and experimental philosophy. His talents in these fields earned him a Fellowship of the Royal Society in 1702 and during the period from 1697 to 1735 he made many contributions to the publications of the Royal Society. From his correspondence it is obvious that Derham moved in elevated circles, both in the church and with the scientists of the day, including Sir Isaac Newton. Other honours bestowed upon him included an invitation to preach sermons at the church of St Mary-le-Bow, Cheapside and he undertook this pleasant task on 16 occasions. Derham was also Chaplain to George, Prince of Wales, and George I made him a Canon at Windsor Castle, into which he was installed in 1716 at the age of 59. The University of Oxford remembered their old graduate by conferring upon him, in 1730, the degree of Doctor of Divinity by Diploma for his services to religion and science.

Following the death of his first wife, William Derham remarried in 1699 to Anna Scott of Woolstan

Engrav'd by Jos.h Baker.

William Derham

Hall, Chigwell; they had three daughters and two sons.

In the year of his remarriage, besides fulfilling his parish duties, Derham found time to conduct weather observations in Upminster and wrote to a friend, including various data concerned with wind direction, cloud formations, barometer and thermometer readings and also levels of rainfall. He used the church tower as his observatory and on the south side of the wooden tower there was a door opening upon a stage from which it is said that Dr Derham could see the shipping on the Thames, as the trees between Upminster and the river were not very high about 1700.

Dr Derham was one of the first men to discover the speed of sound. He undertook experiments using the guns at Woolwich and also those at Belhus Park, Aveley. He discovered that the sound of gunfire at Woolwich, a distance of 12 miles as the crow flies, took 56 seconds to reach Upminster and another experiment showed that the sound of the bells at Hornchurch church took $4\frac{1}{2}$ seconds to arrive at Upminster. He worked out that the speed of sound was 1,125 feet per second. Emminent men, including Newton, subsequently confirmed that Derham's original calculation was only a few feet out, although the speed of sound also depends on the temperature at the time.

William Derham was a copious writer, his best-known work being *The Artificial Clockmaker*. Anyone interested in horology will know that this work on the subject of watch and clockwork was the first authoritative publication on the subject. The first edition was published in 1696, containing 132 pages. By 1736 it was in its 4th edition and had been translated into French and German. Derham's book never ceased to attract attention and even in 1922 a trade publication called *The Dial* was reprinting extracts of his book, first published two hundred years before. The word 'artificial' in the title does not have the same meaning as it does today: William Derham's word meant 'theoretical' or 'mathematical' and the book was about the construction of a clock and the mathematics involved. The book contains the first technical description of clocks and watches and was intended for craftsmen and apprentices.

William Derham's other major works were

Miscellanea Curiosa, 1705, a collection of articles covering the fields of science, mathematics and travel; *Physico-Theology,* 1713, "a demonstration of the being and attributes of God from the works of Creation"; *Astro-Theology,* 1714, "a demonstration of the being and attributes of God from a survey of the heavens"; *Christo-Theology,* 1730, "a demonstration of the Divine Authority of the Christian religion"; *A Defence of the Church's Right in the Leasehold Estate,* 1731, a pamphlet of 32 pages defending the church's method of letting leases to tenants; *Philosophical Experiments and Observations of the late eminent Doctor Robert Hooke FRS and the Geom. Prof. Gresh,* 1726; and *Select Remains of the learned John Ray MA & FRS,* 1760, published after Derham's death by his nephew, George Scott: John Ray was a botanist friend of Derham living at Black Notley.

In addition to the individual works mentioned above William Derham contributed to books on natural history and, in particular, those on English birds and insects. His own especial interest was insects and his personal collection included the majority of known British insects. He also had a fine collection of stuffed birds, once again including most British species.

William Derham died in 1735 and it is clear that this man, although making no spectacular discoveries, contributed to the work undertaken in those days in the fields of science and natural history. His writing tried to show the work of God in everything from the stars to the smallest insect of nature. A learned man who must have overawed the average resident of Upminster with his intellect and his connections in high places, but obviously a man who could revert to his function as a village rector, making contact with the most humble of parishioners.

Samuel Bradshaw followed Derham as rector, but, like his predecessor, he could not live in the rectory due to its state of disrepair. Although a new rectory was built in 1765 Bradshaw only lived in the building for three years before he died. This new rectory was originally moated and Wilson writes that until 1810 about 40 yards of the moat remained on the north side and a portion could also be seen at the southwest corner of the lawn. The original moat was 30 feet wide and 400 feet long on the north and south sides and 200 feet long on the east and west. On the north the bank was parallel with St Mary's Lane and on this side was a bathing house. In 1810 John Rose Holden was rector and had the majority of the moat filled in to build a new approach to the rectory from St Mary's Lane. At that time the rectory grounds contained a small farm. The glebe land totalled 22 acres and on this there was a spacious tithe barn and two cottages for farm workers.

Before the John Rose Holden above, his father, of the same name, had been rector from 1780 to 1799, following the purchase of the advowson by his father William Holden, who was not, though, a rector of Upminster. The earlier John Rose had various arguments with his parishioners, including a difference of opinion as to who should appoint churchwardens. Previously the parish elected one churchwarden from each of the north and south wards. In this dispute the rector won and from then he appointed one warden and the parish elected the other.

The most notable upheaval in the relationship between incumbent and parishioners was on the question of tithes. Back in the Middle Ages the church had always exercised the right to claim one tenth of all that was produced in the parish to go towards the furtherance of the church in the parish. Originally the claim was made by the rector in goods with a visit being made to the farms and smallholdings to claim his one tenth of the harvest or livestock. Over the years many of the parishioners who did not wish to part with their crops or stock arranged with the rector a payment in cash in lieu of the one tenth claim. Even in the latter part of the 18th century there was inflation and Rector Holden realised that the real value of his tithe income was reducing as prices went up, but his cash income remained the same. He therefore gave a year's notice in May, 1798, that in the May of the following year he would revert to the payment of tithes in kind for those previously paying cash. A certain amount of ill-feeling was generated by this announcement, which lasted for the full year, but fortunately for the village he tendered his resignation on the very day that the new arrangement was to take effect.

The second John Rose Holden then took over the living and, being a young man of only 27, he was very keen to carry through his father's ideas about the collection of tithes, not only for his own benefit, but to protect the living of the church. The parishioners soon realised that the new rector was prepared to enforce his father's directive of the year previous, as he was seen walking the farms of the parish counting the sheep and cattle. The farmers therefore met at the 'Bell' Inn to discuss their plan of campaign and, for a start, tried to persuade the rector that he could not change the system, but he would not wear this line of argument. Their next ploy was to offer a lump sum of £610 in lieu of all the tithes, but this was rejected as well. By the summer of 1799 the dispute had really hotted up, with the rector helping himself to his tithes without consulting the owner. The rector then leased the right to collect the tithes to a Mr William Winton Edwards for the sum of £700, which was not much more than he had turned down from the farmers. It was left to Edwards to collect the tithes as best he could and convert the produce or livestock into cash. The methods employed by Edwards and his men were less than gentlemanly, which, naturally, caused more antagonism in the parish. The tithe war continued for some years with Edwards doing his best to recoup his out-lay, but eventually he took the rector to court because he could not claim his full tithes due to the bad feeling generally when the new arrangement was started. Fortunately the whole matter was brought to a conclusion when the Tithe Commutation Act of 1836 did away with tithes in kind and assessed the rector's income as an annual cash figure, which in Upminster's case was £1,052 in 1842.

This second John Rose Holden was rector for 63 years and, although the tithe problem was a long and bitter struggle, it only formed a small part of Holden's term of office, which on the whole was well received by the average parishioner. Writings show he was involved with most aspects of village life and did much for the community at large. Major alterations were planned for the church during his term of office and the estimate for the work was £1,278. The rector himself gave £1,000 towards this figure, a very large amount for those days, and maybe he had mellowed in his old age and wished to make amends for the antagonism he had caused many years earlier.

The living passed in 1862 to J R Holden's nephew, Philip Melancthon Holden, who struck an imposing figure in the village with his flowing white beard and powerful voice. Philip Holden held the living until 1904, when he was succeeded by Hyla Henry Holden, who saw the change from a village community of about 2,000 people to a London suburb of well over 5,000 in 1944. During that time the rector was involved in aspects of the community that had not been seen before. Hyla Henry Holden was a Parish Councillor of the Romford Rural District and was Captain of the Upminster Fire Brigade for a time. He was also involved with youth and sport in the parish, being Captain of the Cricket Club in 1905, for example.

The role of the church in the affairs of the parish had changed tremendously during the time of the Holdens. In 1894 the Local Government Act was passed, taking away from the church the last of their powers in the village and substituting an elected Parish Council. The Parish Council lasted until 1934 when Upminster and Cranham parishes were merged into Hornchurch Urban District Council.

The parish church in most communities is probably the only building that has part of its structure dating back to medieval times or beyond. The age of the building, coupled with the succession of rectors that influenced the lives of their flock through the centuries, makes the parish church, and St Laurence is no exception, one of the most important subjects in the history of a village. Upminster's parish church certainly has a wealth of history connected with the building and the rectors themselves can be seen as individuals, both eminent, like William Derham, and controversial, like the Holdens.

Rectors of St Laurence, Upminster

About 1250	John de Termentre	1397	Robert Keynson
1324	Thomas de Arderne	1397	Henry Charwalton
1328	Adam de Arderne	1401	Peter Hynewyk
1329	Robert de Arderne	1410	William Bildeston
1336	William de Sancto Marco	-	Rob. Wandesforth
1343	John de Hawkesworthe	1437	Ste. German
1354	Thomas de Stanes	-	Will. Okebourne
About 1373	John Brunne	1455	Ric. Brounne

1467	Tho. Swyft	1646-60	Marmaduke James
1470	Ste. Hellard		Reuben Easthorpe
1472	Nic. Sylvester		Edward Green
1479	Will. Lawe		John Robotham
1479	Joh. Carthwaite	1660	John Halke
1482	Ric. Cranwell	1662	John Newton
1483	Guido Ardern	1679	Strangford Viall
1485	Will. Hill	1686	William Bray
1488	Will. Styward	1689	William Derham
1492	Joh. Docwray	1735	Samuel Bradshaw
1535	Rob. Downing	1768	James Bingham
1537	Edw. Keble	1770	John William Hopkins
1554	Rob. Dent	1780	John Rose Holden
1557	Joh. Leder	1799	John Rose Holden, M.A.
1562	William Washer	1862	Philip Melancthon Holden
1609	John Bowle	1904	Hyla Henry Holden, M.A.
1614	William Halke	1944	Hyla Rose Holden
1615	Michael Halke	1971	Maurice Harper
1625	Chris. Denne	1986	Stanley Swift
1638	John Halke		

St Laurence Church, 1793

Drawn by I C Barrow
Essex Record Office

ECONOMIC HISTORY

At the time of the Domesday survey all the inhabitants of Upminster worked on one or other of the two manors and were engaged in looking after the manors' sheep and swine and also working in the woods, cutting trees and clearing the woodland for cultivation. Gradually the woodland decreased and sheep rearing predominated, especially near the Commons in the north and the south of the parish, with arable farming concentrated nearer the centre of the village. Various published wills and inventories mention bequests of sheep in the 15th century and it was noted earlier that the rector held sheep in the 1550s. By the 17th century there was a variety of agriculture encompassing all the different crops and livestock, as well as orchards and the making of cheese and ale.

The common land was used extensively for pasturing sheep and in the south Chafford Heath, lying either side of Bramble Lane, gave six acres of pasture for the tenants of Gaynes manor. The common had been used for this purpose in the 1770s, but had been enclosed by the 1840s. Earlier note has been made of the two commons in the north of the parish - Tylers Common on the east of Nag's Head Lane, providing 78 acres of common grazing land, and Upminster Common to the west, which had slightly less land for the local villagers' use. During World War II Tylers Common, by then the only remaining, had been requisitioned by the Essex War Agricultural Committee for the growing of crops and in 1950 Essex County Council tried to enclose the common to continue its use for this purpose. Local opposition, with the aid of the Ministry of Agriculture, over-ruled this decision and the local residents, notably Edward Luther, who campaigned to protect the common for anyone to enjoy today deserve our thanks. Upminster Common was enclosed by agreement in 1846/9 and comprised 70 acres.

Upminster land usage by acres

Year	Arable	Pasture	Woods, Commons, Roads & Homes
1795	2700	450	400
1842	2000	1000	400
1905	1600	1050	750
1925	1030	970	1400
1961	1250	450	1700

The above chart shows the comparison between the acreages of arable and pastureland, with a gradual decline in arable, although pasture increased in the 19th century when sheep farming was so popular. Latterly both categories have decreased as land was converted into residential use, although the acreage of market gardening, included in the last column, has increased in the 20th century.

Upminster's population figures over a thousand years are –

Year	Population	Number of houses	Number of families	Number in families
1086	150		35/40	
1695	370	60		6.1
1777	550/600			
1801	765	123		
1811	929	149	162	5.7 *
1821	952	166	174	5.5
1831	1033	186	202	5.1
1841	1117	215		
1851	1228	244		
1861	1342	274		
1871	1329	282	283	4.7
1881	1202 †	280	299	4.0
1891	1409	309	322	4.4
1901	1477	315	323	4.6
1911	2468 +		553	4.4
1921	3559		870	4.1
1931	5732		1536	3.7
1951	13038		4288	3.0
1961	11676 =		4020	2.9 *

* The size of families reduced over the centuries with a drastic
slump from 5.7 in 1811 to 2.9 in 1961.
† Population falls slightly from 1861 to 1881.
+ The Census Report comments "The large increase in the population
of Upminster is attributable mainly to its development as a Garden
City." The total population includes a branch of the County Lunatic
Asylum, as it was called in 1911, which was sited at Harold Court,
where the inmates and staff totalled 77.
= Boundary changes reduced Upminster's area from 3,375 acres to
2,679.

It can be seen that Upminster's population grew
very slowly until the housing developments started this
century, for, of course, everyone was employed on the
land and the village could support only so many people on
the available acreage. Upminster did not have a brewery,
a tannery or an ironworks, like Hornchurch, to give
villagers alternative employment to the land, but there
was a thriving brick and tile works for a period and also
the two windmills, which would have given a number of
villagers work.

The mill on Upminster, or Gaynes, Common was of
the post mill type and its location, according to Chapman
& Andre's 1777 map was just to the north of Shepherds'
Hill, where Ivy Lodge Farm is today. The exact date of
its construction is not known, but it may have been in
existence in 1665 when Thomas Dawson, a miller, was
buried in Upminster churchyard. The Pinchon family were
millers there in the 1770s and were still there in 1846. In
1826 two of the sails were blown off in a storm, which
in turn destroyed a barn some distance away. The story
of this storm also relates that a man was blown up into
a tree, but was none the worse for his experience. In
1875 David Pinchon sold the windmill, which was pulled
down in 1882.

Upminster's second windmill is the well-known landmark at the top of Upminster Hill and it is fortunate
that so much is known about the mill, its construction
and the millers that ran the business for about 130 years.
It will be recalled that in 1800 William Nokes was the
tenant farmer of Bridge House, the freehold being owned
by Richard Harding Newman of Nelmes Manor, Hornchurch. At the time his brother, James Nokes, was the
tenant of Hunt's Farm, Corbets Tey Road. The Parish

Rate Book shows that there was an adjustment to the
rateable value of the land worked by William and James
Nokes indicating that the land on the north side of
Upminster Hill in the Bridge House acreage was transferred from William to James, who in 1803 built his windmill and its ancillary buildings on top of the hill, together
with a bakery and cottages fronting Hall Lane (Station
Road).

The mill prospered and, by 1812, the rateable value
had increased from £30 to £77, showing that by this time
James had added his steam engine house to drive the sails
when there was no wind. On James Nokes' death in 1838
the windmill passed to his brother, William, who himself
died eight years later. The ownership then passed to
James' son, Thomas, who also inherited Bridge House
Farm. By 1849 the whole estate was so heavily in debt
that it was put up for auction, realising the sum of
£2,000. The purchaser was Ambrose Colson of South
Weald, who then sold the estate to James Wadeson. The
sale bill at the auction described the mill estate as a
substantial corn mill capable of dealing with a large
amount of business. The ancillary buildings were made up
of an engine house, granaries, stabling and other outbuildings. The adjacent house was a detached residence
built about 1840: there were two reception rooms, break-
fast parlour, kitchen, 5 bedrooms and w.c., in the base-
ment there was a coal, wood and wine cellar. Nearby
there were two millers' cottages, one having three rooms,
the other two. There was also a large elongated pond,
which must have been unusual in view of its position on
the top of a substantial hill.

Whilst Thomas Nokes was running the mill he had,
as his foreman, Thomas Abraham, who originally lived in
the Upminster area with his uncle, John Arkell, who
farmed at South Ockendon. Abraham first worked for
Thomas Nokes as carman and later was foreman at the
West Thurrock Mills before taking a similar post at
Upminster. When the estate came up for auction Thomas
Abraham had the chance to buy the mill, but didn't. A
mill foreman's pay was not high and in the following
years he moved back to farming at Cranham and then at
Orsett. Obviously milling was his calling, for his next job
was managing the mill at Navestock. James Wadeson, the

new owner, offered him the mill estate again in September, 1857, for £1,900, but Thomas Abraham did not buy the whole estate, but only the mill and the surrounding land for £1,100, of which he borrowed £500. Gradually, after a long period during which the mill and its business had been run down, Abraham built the mill up again into a going concern. Thomas died in 1882 and he was succeeded by his younger son, John Arkell Abraham, the elder son, Thomas, not wishing to take over the mill. John had been born in 1830 and also had much experience in milling before joining his father at Upminster.

During John Abraham's ownership the mill was twice damaged by storms. The *Essex Herald* reported that in September, 1889, lightning struck one of the top sails, ripping it to pieces and scattering bits of the sail over a fifty yard area. It looks as if lightning struck twice in this storm, for the report mentions that lightning also travelled down the sail chain fusing the links together. Ten years later a very strong wind exerted so much pressure on the sails that the iron shaft to which the sails were fixed snapped and the four sails crashed to the ground, bringing with them large amounts of wood and ironwork. The residents of Upminster came to John Abraham's rescue by contributing £200 towards the cost of repairs and this reflected the high regard in which he was held in the village.

John Abraham was a founder member of Upminster Cricket Club and offered himself for election on the first Upminster Parish Council, although he did not get a seat. John Abraham died in 1912 and, not having married, the business was left to his two nephews, Alfred and Clement. Unfortunately the business was soon to decline due to much larger mills and more modern methods, making wind mills an uneconomic venture. The 1914-18 War did not help, as there was less corn to grind and, consequently, as the mill was under-utilised it was no longer profitable. The death knell of the business came on 25th March, 1927, when a strong wind ripped off the fan, scattering pieces into Highview Gardens, which had been built following sale of land belonging to the mill. The windmill had not been used for the whole of that winter and work had just been started on repairs. A report at the time said that Mr Abraham doubted whether the damage would

The Windmill, 1949

Photograph by K O Jones

be repaired, as he had been putting the mill back into working order for sentimental reasons only, as grinding these days did not pay.

The mill had withstood the ravages of the weather and the changes seen in the economy over 130 years and when the Abraham family sold the mill in 1934 they probably thought it would be demolished, as had been the fate of many other mills about this time. The mill and its land were bought for £3,400 by W H Simmons of Upminster for residential development, although he intended to preserve the mill itself. Three years later, though, the mill was on the market again and this time the purchaser was Essex County Council, who again intended to develop the site and demolish the mill. The *Romford Recorder* published a report of the public outcry at the latter proposal and the County Council changed its mind. During World War II nothing was done in the way of repair and the mill's condition deteriorated quickly. In 1946 the mill was surveyed and the cost of repairs was estimated at £400. Local residents must take a fair deal of the credit for saving the mill for, following a public meeting in 1948, a Windmill Committee was formed to raise funds to effect repairs. The Committee took a lease from the County Council to enable them to have access to the mill and gained the support of the Society for the Protection of Ancient Buildings, who backed their appeal for funds. There was also formed the Friends of the Mill, a body whose aims were similar to the Windmill Committee, and whose annual subscription was five shillings. Despite much support the overall situation did not improve. By 1959 repairs costing £600 had been carried out, but the mill did not look any better for the expenditure. However, in 1960 the Essex County Council took more positive action than they had in the 23 years they had owned the mill. The Council spent £4,000 demolishing the mill house, steam plant and outbuildings and levelling the site. They then spent £2,000 on major repairs to the mill itself, rebuilding the lower gantry, painting the outside and making the building weather and vandal proof.

With the reorganisation of local government Upminster moved out of the County of Essex and into the London Borough of Havering to whom the ownership of the mill now passed. The new Borough continued the good work started by the County and further sums were spent to enable the mill to open to visitors. The mill opened its doors to the public in September, 1967, and has been open at regular intervals each summer since, in conjunction with the Hornchurch & District Historical Society.

Most of the early windmills, right back to the 13th century, were Post Mills. This was virtually a wooden box, housing the machinery and topped by the sails. The sails were fixed to the body and consequently the whole mill had to be turned to face the wind. As, therefore, the priority was weight, so that mill could be turned as easily as possible, the structure was invariably quite small: a local mill of this design is at Mountnessing. In the 14th century Tower Mills were developed, consisting of a fixed brick or stone tower body with sails fixed to a revolving cap. From this style developed the Smock Mill, of which Upminster's is an excellent example. Instead of a square brick or stone body, the base was made of wood standing on a brick base. Usually the mill was eight sided with the body tapering upwards and looking like the smock worn by country folk many years ago.

The mechanics of the working of the mill are well documented in Anthony Butler's book *Upminster Mill*, but a few of the salient features should be mentioned. The smock mill, as has been said, has a cap at the top to which the sails are fixed, which revolves to catch the wind. On top of the cap is the fantail, which is a mini-windmill of 6 wooden vanes set at right angles to the main sails. The wind strikes the fantail and, by a system of gears, the cap is turned so that the main sails face into the wind. The sails themselves can be adjusted like those of a sailing boat to take all the wind or spill some of it if it is too strong. All the way down each sail are shutters that can be adjusted like Venetian blinds to any angle required: they are connected on a rod and all move together automatically when the pressure is too great, so enabling the machinery inside to be kept at a fairly constant speed.

The interior is divided into 5 floors, connected by stairs with the various levels having names like bin floor, stone floor and meal floor. A description of the machinery on each floor and the uses made of it can be found in Anthony Butler's book. Mention has been made of the steam plant adjacent to the mill, which aided the grinding when there was no wind. It seems that this plant was built only about 8 years after the mill itself was built in 1803 and the building and tall chimney were not demolished until 1960. The steam engine is said to have come from a Thames steamboat and the boiler was made by Davey Paxman of Colchester. The drive shaft leading from the steam plant into the mill was 50 feet long and it is said that it took the best part of a day to get up enough steam to drive the mill machinery. The engine was taken away in 1940 and the machinery went when the steam plant was demolished in 1960.

Those interested in the windmill should visit the Central Library in Romford, where there is a very large model of Upminster's windmill. It is 7'6" high and was made by Mr E W King, who lived in Highview Gardens, very near the mill itself. The model works and every detail is a reproduction of the original.

Many drawings, paintings and sketches have been made of the mill, which is truly a magnificent example of an English Smock Mill. It featured on a London Transport poster in 1967 when advertising a leaflet *Mills   in and around London*.

Although the windmills did not employ many people directly they were a very important part of the farming community, 65% of the population in the early 19th century being engaged in agriculture and, earlier, this percentage would have been higher still.

There was a tannery at Corbets Tey certainly between the years 1573 and 1635 when references to Upminster's tanner appear in local records. From the 18th century gravel extraction has been in operation, especially in the southern part of the parish and this must have given work for numerous residents, as the gravel would have been dug out by hand. The only other industry in Upminster where a workforce of any number was employed was that of brick and tile making.

On the extreme northeast boundary of the parish Brick House Farm was the site of an early brickfield. Wilson mentions in his 1856 book that, although the brick-fields had not been used for many years, the kiln was visible, though crumbling away. Slightly south of Brick House Farm is Tylers Farm, which in Anglo-Saxon means 'tile earth wood', indicating that this also was the site of another long-gone brick and tile works. Moving even further south, the most well-known of Upminster's brick-fields was near the junction of Hall Lane and Bird Lane, at the rear of Chapmans Farm.

There was possibly a brick kiln on the Bird Lane site in 1708, when there is reference to Samuel Springham having a house at the brick kilns. It is known that in 1774 Matthew Howland Patrick built his kiln of 45 feet diameter and 70 feet high on this site. The diameter at its summit was 10 feet. Mr Patrick was the lessee of Upminster Hall at the time and husband of the widowed Mrs Branfil. In 1791 Patrick's stepson, Champion Branfil III, spent over £200 improving the site. The kiln made bricks, tiles and pipes and was worked by a succession of lessees, including Messrs Wilson & Hook in the 1880s. The museum at the Tithe Barn contains examples of this firm's work and also that of subsequent brickmakers.

The kiln's most productive phase was when James Brown bought the lease. Brown also had works at Braintree and Chelmsford, with a wharf at Whitechapel and a Head Office in London. Towards the end of the 19th century he had also acquired sites at Boreham, Writtle and Brentwood, but later he concentrated his activities at Upminster and Brentwood. James Brown enlarged the site after he bought the lease in 1880 and also provided work-men's cottages, which can still be seen in Bird Lane and are still known by their original names of Plain Tile and Pan Tile Cottages, referring to the type of tile used on their roofs. These roof tiles are still in place and a small expedition is recommended to look at these cottages and to spot the location of the brickfields themselves. A map of the turn of the century shows the plan of the brick-works in some detail: they were on the north side of Bird Lane, extending down to where the Southend Road (A127) is now and, after their acquisition by Brown, he developed the field south of Bird Lane by building a new kiln and extending the works to where Dart Close and Fleet Avenue are now. The map also shows a railway line leading to Upminster Station, a horse-drawn two-foot narrow guage affair that went along the back of Upminster Hall and Holden Way and Claremont Gardens, crossing Deyncourt Gardens at the bottom of that road and thence into the railway sidings. Originally, after passing Upminster Hall, the line had turned directly south-west to Upminster Station, but it was re-routed after Deyncourt Gardens was built. In Bird Lane there is still a piece of railway line above the tarmac as it crosses the road from one side of the works to the other.

At its peak the brickworks employed about 20 men and there were also some one-storey cottages on the north side of Bird Lane for itinerant workmen. These cottages, together with other small buildings, are now in ruins just off Bird Lane, but the works on the south side are all lost in the new wood that has grown up around them behind the veterinary surgery in Hall Lane (Olympique House). This southern site still has a few old brick walls and interesting shaped bricks made on the site can sometimes be found. The main entrance to the works in James Brown's time (1880-1917) was up the Chase, between the last house in Hall Lane on the east side and just before Olympique House when approaching the site from Upminster Station. The gateway is still there and is marked accordingly.

The original kiln in the north field was known locally as 'The Dome' and the clay in this area was particularly suitable for fancy work, such as ornamental tiles and chimney pots. The kiln in the south field was known as 'The Shaft' and it would appear that the majority of bricks made left the area by way of Upminster Station, with few houses being built of locally made bricks. Apart from the cottages James Brown built for his own workmen, the only building of local brick seems to be Upminster Court, built in 1906. Little is known of the last years of this local industry, but the business began to decline after the departure of James Brown. The Upminster United Brick Works, Ltd., owned by Mr Beck, operated the works until 1929, but local strikes forced him to discontinue. In the early 1930s the Essex Brick & Tile Co., Ltd., were on the scene, but this company went into voluntary liquidation in 1933.

Although mechanisation existed inside the brick-works buildings, outside in the clay pits the labourers toiled digging the clay out by hand. A labourer would pull an empty truck down into the pit and, after filling it up with clay, it would be hauled up again by someone with a horse. The trucks were 'V' shaped and could be tipped either way. Apart from the main railway track from the works to Upminster Station various branch lines were linked to the clay pits to assist with the hauling of clay to the works. These short lines were of a temporary nature and often changed around as clay digging moved from one location to another. It seems the pits rarely flooded, which is surprising for clay, and this was attributable to a layer of gravel that lay 20/30 feet below the level of the southern field. The clay after extraction was laid out to weather and then the stones had to be removed. The clay was then washed and ground in a mill by a small steam engine. The bricks were moulded into shape either by hand with wooden moulds or by machine with metal moulds. Probably the less used shapes were moulded by hand. Apart from the standard shaped bricks recognised today James Brown in his time manufactured all the different shapes and sizes of special bricks used at the turn of the century. A copy of James Brown's trade catalogue of 1900 is held at the Essex Record Office. The drawings show those found on the site with their numbers indicating that the firm had a very extensive range. After manufacture the bricks were put into box trucks and hauled by horse along the track to Upminster Station, the trucks being filled with coal for the kilns for the return journey. Alternatively the bricks were taken by horse and cart out through the Chase exit into Hall Lane and down to the Station or direct to the purchaser.

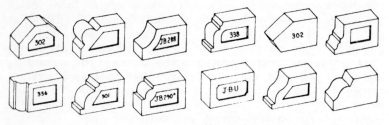

THE MEDIEVAL RECORDS

In Chapter One it was seen that the manor of Upminster Hall had been retained by Waltham Abbey after the Conquest and the monks appeared to have gone about their business uninterrupted for nearly five hundred years until Henry VIII dissolved the monasteries in 1536. Morant in his *History of Essex* of 1768 described Upminster Hall in the Middle Ages as probably a retiring place or hunting seat for the Abbot. Very few references for this period in Upminster Hall's history are found, although there is a very early entry in the Calendar of Close Rolls for 1190, when Richard I granted the Abbey the right to enclose 104 acres of land, apparently already taken by the monks previously. The Close Rolls were so called because of their comparitively private nature and, being addressed to a particular person, the document was folded small and secured by a narrow strip of parchment, having the great seal placed thereon. The original document was issued by the Lord Chancellor in the name of the sovereign and was either sent back to the Chancery with a return of the proceedings or sometimes retained by the person to whom it was directed with a copy remaining in official custody.

There are many more references to Gaynes Manor, as we now know it, although in the Middle Ages it does not appear to have had a name. The various references just describe the manor as the manor at Upminster and, although there was Upminster Hall as well, this was held by the church and chroniclers did not feel there would be any misunderstanding. The Gaynes manor eventually took its name from the Engayne family the first of whom to hold the property being Vitalis Engayne. One of his sons was called Henry, who inherited the manor in the reign of Henry III. An entry in the Calendar of Inquisitions, recording matters dealing with the hereditary descent of land, refers to Henry Engayne putting his age "variously stated as 30, 30 or more, and 35". It looks as if at this time the Engayne family held land in Huntingdon, Cambridge, Northampton, Hertford, Suffolk, Somerset and Essex. Henry's father, Vitalis, was probably a Minister of State for Henry III (1216–72), as letters written to Henry by the King refer to matters of national importance and this is why the family held so much land. After relating Henry's rough age and land holdings, the entry then goes as follows –

"Upmenistre, land and advowson which does no service because the manors of Worthe (Worle, Somerset) and Upmenistre defend themselves against the King by service of 1½ knights fee." 'Knights fee' relates to a level of taxation levied upon a manor by the King. When Vitalis Engayne held the manor by military tenure he was obliged to provide the King with soldiers and equipment according to the extent of his land. Vitalis was summoned in this way in 1242. When his son inherited the land with the levy of 1½ knight's fee it appeared that, by then, it had become a measure of taxation. The King, when needing funds for the Exchequer, would levy a rate of so many pounds per knight's fee. Not very different from the rating system we have today whereby the larger the property you own the more you pay.

The next entry in respect of Gaynes is in the Patent Rolls. This category of entry is so called because they are of a public nature and usually addressed to all persons and concern matters relating to grants, liberties, privileges, lands and pensions. Henry had died unmarried and the manor passed to his brother, Sir John, and from him to his son, John. The Patent Rolls of 1297 record –

"Westminster, 12 July, 1297. Licence for John Engayne who is going with the King beyond seas, so enfeoff [lease] Simon de Havering of the manor of Upmenstre, Essex, which he holds in chief, saving the advowson of the church, to hold the said John and Elinor his wife and their heirs for ever at a rent after the expiration of ten years of £10 a year."

So the manor was leased to Simon de Havering rent free for the first ten years and the £10 a year afterwards.

John de Engayne died in 1302 and the Calendar of

Inquisitions and Post Mortems records a writ enquiring what lands John held of the King on the day he died. All land still belonged to the King and John was the chief tenant, although the report back referring to the manor said, "He at one time held the manor of the King in chief by a Knight's fee of the honour of Mongomeri, but he did not die seized thereof, Simon de Haverynge now holds it". Later in the 14th century Sir Thomas Engayne was tenant in chief, but, once again, the manor was leased to others. The Calendar of Close Rolls records in 1369, after Sir Thomas' death, a rent of a pair of gilt spurs price six pence to be paid to the manor of Upminster to Katherine, widow of Thomas Engayne.

Earlier it was noted how Alice Perrers' fortunes had fluctuated. She had had much influence over Edward III before his death, receiving many gifts from the King in way of land and money. She became rich and powerful and, although banished in 1376 and 1377, returned shortly afterwards having married Sir William Windsore, Deputy of Ireland. In the Patent Rolls for 15th March, 1380, there is the following –

"Grant in fee simple to William de Wyndsore who had married Alice de Perrers of lands and tenements which she acquired whilst single and those which others acquired to her use, forfeited by the Judgement of Parliament against her... [all her estates are then mentioned, including the manor of Upmynstre]... after the death of Lora, wife of William Morewode and late lands of John de Havering..."

Sir William Windsore died in 1384 and Alice de Perrers lived at Gaynes until her death in 1400. Alice was buried in Upminster Church and the record of her will makes interesting reading as it tells a little of her family. The will directed that she be buried on the north side before the altar of Our Lady the Virgin, which is now the Esdaile Chapel. She gave the church an oxen, together with money to buy candles to burn around her body and also to buy ornaments for the church. Other bequests were –

- for the repairing of the highway, 40 shillings
- for the poor 10 marks on burying and 20 shillings for the poor of Upminster
- for the Chaplain, 6 marks

- John Pelham, sacrist (sexton), three shillings and four pence
- to Joane, my youngest daughter my manor of Gaynes
- to Jane and Joane, my daughters, all my other manors which John Wyndsore usurped, which I desire my heirs and executors to recover...

During this period there was much legal wrangling over the ownership of Gaynes. The laws of succession and inheritance were, of course, observed, but with the King still the ultimate owner of the estate bequests by the Crown could often upset parties who thought they were entitled to the property. Sir William Windsore had been granted the reversion of Gaynes manor as a reward for doing military service overseas, his wife having held the manor previously while single. Then Alice Perrers inherited the estate, so she thought, and she in turn left it to her daughter, Joane. Apparently, though, the King had granted the reversion of Gaynes to Sir John Deyncourt, who died in 1393, leaving as his heir Roger Deyncourt, who was a minor. Consequently, when Alice Perrers was living at Gaynes after the death of her husband, William Windsore, she was not really the owner (after the King) of Gaynes. With Roger Deyncourt being a minor the estate reverted to the King's control until he was old enough to take over the estate for himself. During this period of Roger's minority the estate was looked after by Conan Fitz-Henry on the King's behalf. The Calendar of Fine Rolls in 1402, in the reign of the new King, Henry IV, recorded the trusteeship -

"Committant to Conan Fitz-Henry by mainprise [entrusted] of the keeping of the manor of Upmynstre which is held of the King... the said manor now in the King's hand by the death of the said Lora [wife of William Morewode] and by the death of the said John [Deyncourt] and by reason of the minority of Roger Deyncourt..."

When the trustees changed in 1403, the entry in the Rolls added that "... they maintain the house and buildings pertaining to the manor, and support all charges incumbent on it".

The trustees appear to have done their job in looking after the land and buildings as two entries in the

Calendar of Inquisitions demonstrate. Apparently following the death of Lora Morewode in 1393 Robert Chychele of London took possession of two properties on the manor estate called Napers tenement and Snellyggestenement and land belonging to the estate worth 40 shillings a year. When occupying the properties and land he kept the profits generated instead of passing them to the King, there being no Lord of the Manor at that time.

During the period of Roger Deyncourt's minority Alice Perrers' daughter, Joane, made many petitions to the Crown concerning her inheritance of Gaynes manor. The Calendar of Close Rolls records these, culminating in 1406 in a settlement of 40 marks a year for life to surrender all claims to the estate in favour of the minor, Roger Deyncourt. The settlement records that if she or her attorney is not present at the church to receive the settlement then it should be paid to the rector or church-warden to hold on her behalf. If, though, the Lord of the Manor is 40 days in arrears in paying the settlement then she may enter the estate again and hold the property on the payment of 100 shillings a year, with the proviso that she pay nothing until the settlement arrears are paid. The settlement was made and acknowledged on 27th November, 1406.

In 1419 the Close Rolls finally recorded that the King's hand was removed from Gaynes and the manor came into the possession of Roger Deyncourt. This meant that Roger became the freeholder and absolute owner of the estate, being no longer required to supply the King with 'knight's fee' or any form of rate in lieu. An entry in the Fine Rolls of 1428 mentions Roger Deyncourt being appointed, with seven others, to collect on behalf of the Crown within the County of Essex six shillings and eight pence from all inhabitants who were householders (this appears to be some form of county rate!).

Roger Deyncourt died in 1455 and for the next hundred years all seemed peace and quiet at Gaynes Manor, despite the Wars of the Roses being fought else-where in the country. In London the great land barons were becoming a dying breed and in their place rose the wealthy merchants and professional men. Nicholas Wayte, who was a draper, came to Upminster from London and lived at Gaynes until he died in 1543. The Wayte family had no children and the manor was sold to Ralph Latham, a goldsmith from London that same year. The Court Rolls record the obtaining of a licence to transfer the estate that May into Ralph Latham's name: the estate comprised the manor house, three other houses, 500 acres of arable land, 40 acres of meadow, 200 acres of pasture, 200 acres of woodland and 60 acres of furze and heath in Upminster and Hornchurch. This transaction was quickly followed, on 7th July, 1543, by the purchase for £848.18.11d. of the lordship and manor of Upminster Hall, which had come on the market by virtue of Henry VIII's dissolution of the monasteries. Ralph Latham now owned a very large proportion of the village. The villagers must have wondered if these dramatic changes coming so soon one after the other would effect their lives, for so many relied on the manors for their livelihood.

After Ralph Latham's death, his son, William, inherited the estates and an entry in the Patent Rolls of 1564 shows the extent of land owned by the family. The granting of a licence in that year refers to the manors of Gaynes and Upminster Hall, together with lands in "Horne churche, Craneham, Great Warley, Alveley, Stifford, Dagnam, Southokingdon, Northockingdon and Havering". The Lathams must have owned quite a few thousand acres in southwest Essex, their holding in Upminster alone probably exceeding two thousand.

For another 80 years all was tranquil in Upminster, for there are no entries in any of the Court Rolls relating to the two manors. Either things were peaceful or the Latham family had such a firm hold on the village that no-one was prepared to cause any problems. Not until 1645 is there another entry and this refers to a feud in the family, probably reflecting the troubled times the country was experiencing. Charles I was faced with open conflict with Parliament that eventually resulted in the Civil War and his own execution. On 6th June, 1645, a deposition was lodged by William Latham, son of the earlier William, that his own son, Ralph, said, "The Devil take Parliament and all the committed for they will undo everyone, and have undone me already." It would appear that Ralph supported the King and his father was a Parliamentarian or otherwise he would not have lodged the deposition against him.

Turning from the Court Rolls and their glimpses of the history of the manors the ordinary inhabitants of the village also figure in records from time to time. An entry in the Patent Rolls for 1265, in the reign of Henry III, records a pardon for William le Meilur who apparently had killed Brice de Upmestre accidentally. In 1324 Thomas de Arden, the parson at 'Uppeministre' was granted protection for a year – one wonders what that was all about! A few years later, in 1344 in Edward III's reign, the Rolls record the appointment of a power of attorney for a villager possibly going abroad to fight for the King. It is surprising that so long ago ordinary people were that educated and sophisticated to be able to appoint someone to act on their behalf when out of the country. It is not certain that the person was an Upminster resident, but the fact that he appointed the parson as his attorney rather indicates that he probably lived in the village. The entry reads –

"John de Haverynton 'Chivaler' [Horseman] going to Ireland in the Kings service with Ralph de Ufford has letters nominating John de Hawkesworthe parson of the church of Upminster and John atte Doune as his attorneys in England for one year."

A few years later there is an entry for 1354 giving an indication of the wild life that abounded in this south-western part of Essex. The Court Rolls record the commissioning of John de Staunton "appointing him to be the surveyor of the King's game as well as herons, partridge and pheasants, cranes and other river fowl, as of hares, foxes, cats and other wild beasts of game in the towns and places of Orsete, Alvithele... Upmynstre... Dakenham Meresh [Marsh], Berkyng Meresh, Stifford and Reynham and to arrest and imprison all destroyers of the same by snares or other engines found there".

Still in the reign of Edward III the Calendar of Close Rolls records in 1367 that an order was passed "to cause John Gylemyn of Upmenstre to have the right to the property in Alvythele held by John Wardayn of Alvythele hanged for felony it is said... after in the hands of the King for a year and a day that John Wardayn held them of the said John Gylemyn by fealty [tenancy] and the service of three shillings and fourpence". It looks as if Wardayn was Gylemyn's tenant and following his execution, the property was held by the Crown for a year before reverting to John Gylemyn, the rent previously being 3s.4d [17p.] a year.

In the early years of the 15th century an Upminster couple named Hugh and Margaret Draper had a son who unfortunately, as is recorded, "from his birth was an idiot and a fool all his life". It looks as if they gave 60 acres of their land called Brokeland in Upminster to the Abbot of Stratford Langthorn and his convent in return, probably, for looking after their son when they died. However, the Drapers had not received permission for this transfer and consequently, as John Draper was still a minor when his parents did die, the land, part of Gaynes manor, passed to the King during the son's minority. Apparently the Abbot was already in possession of the land and taking profits from it since its acquisition and the entry states "that they must answer the King therefore". Later entries reveal that the land was taken out of the Abbot's charge and passed to others who were possibly trustees of the son, although we do not know what happened to him. It is unlikely that the Abbot continued to look after him if the bequest was taken from him.

An Upminster resident who had obviously gone through a worrying time for about eleven years was William atte Hethe, who was pardoned in February, 1407, having previously been accused in May, 1396, of "ravishing Joan, the wife of John Busch of Upminster".

A couple of years later, in 1409, it looks as if some of the villagers were taking the law into their own hands. A dispute had occurred and a writ was issued in June ordering William Brown of Upminster and others to set free William Elys, a tailor, who was being sought by the authorities in respect of a charge brought by John Branfelde and Walter Coke, a butcher. The entry in the Rolls unfortunately does not say with what William Elys was being charged.

It was commented earlier that all was quiet from the mid-15th to mid-16th centuries as regards entries about the two manors and the same can be said for other incidents in the village, until 1555 which was quite an eventful year, for there are two major entries in the Rolls relating to Upminster villagers. Firstly, Christopher

Caterman, butcher of Upminster, received a pardon in February "of all felonies and homicides committed by him before 30th September last, all treason, murders, highway and church robberies, rape and burglaries being accepted, to that he stand to right in the court of King and Queen [reign of Philip and Mary]".

Later in the year, in October, there was a fight involving seven villagers from Upminster, Corbets Tey and Aveley, in which one of their number was killed. The entry in the Patent Rolls recites the affair –

"Whereas Thomas Knott, alias Nott the younger, late of Stubbers in Northeokyngton, County Essex, Gentleman, alias 'Yoman', Robert Askewe late of the same, Gentleman, William Butler, late of the same, Yoman and Thomas Hall, late of Corbetstye in Upminster, County Essex, yoman, alias late of Romford, County Essex, 'horse courser', are indicted for that they on 1st October about 9 a m in the high road called Potspringe Lane in Upminster assaulted with force and arms, namely with swords, etc. and Brybates, of malice aforethought John Barnes of Corbetstye, husbondman, Humfrey Barnes, yoman, and William Hill late of Aveley, County Essex, cowper, and beat and maltreated them, and Hall, with a staff of the price of two pence, gave Hill a mortal wound upon the head three inches in length and two inches in depth, of which wound Hill languished for $2\frac{1}{2}$ hours and died at Bushes in Upminster on the same day."

Surprisingly, the following entry in the Rolls pardons Thomas Knott "of the said felony".

The question of rate demands and rate increases is not exclusive to the 20th century. Way back in 1598 the residents of Upminster were complaining about their rates and took it upon themselves to draw up a petition which found itself entered in the Acts of the Privy Council for 24th February, 1598. Apparently before then the rates were levied according to the wealth of the resident in conjunction with the land held, but the new rating order seemed to dispense with wealth and stick strictly to acreage of land held. This resulted in villagers who were not very wealthy in terms of possessions, but who happened to own a fair amount of land, being rated higher than before and having to pay a lot more than villagers who owned less land, but who had many more material possessions. The entry is reproduced in the original English –

"24 February. Signed as the letter aforegoinge.

"A letter to Sir Henry Graye, Sir Thomas Mildemay and Sir John Petre, knightes, or to any two of them, whereof Sir John Petre to be one. Whereas the inclosed peticion hath bin exhibited unto us by certain of the inhabitantes of the parishe of Upminster in the countie of Essex, wherby they complaine of an overburthensomme taxe imposed on them by a new devised order ratinge them (as they informe us) farre otherwise then hath bin accustomed and to the great disadvantage of the meaner sorte, who being charged according to the number of the acres of grounde that they holde and occupie, and they occupyinge the same (as it is like enoughe) at highe rates, are burthened by this meanes with an unjust proporcion in respect of diverse others that happelie keepe fewer acres of groundes in their occupacion and yet are wealthie men. Foreasmuch as wee holde it not meete that any innovacion be made in these matters of taxes but uppon verie especiall and approved cause, and it cannot but be very meete that the charges uppon suche occasions of her Majesy's service be rated in suche indifferent manner as the richer sorte maie not shifte the burthen from their own shoulders uppon those that are of meaner abilitie, we have therefore thought good to sende the said complaint and peticion hereinclosed unto you that in this tyme of the vacancie of a Lieutenant can best judge thereof and (if it be needfull) take order for redresse, prayinge and requiring you to have consideracion thereof and of suche reasons as the peticioners can alleadge in their owne behalfe, and thereuppon to give direccion to suche as sett the rates for the said parrishe of Upminster to followe the course and forme that hath bin used heretofore, or if you shall finde just and sufficient cause of alteracion, then to certifie us thereof, that the peticioners thereby maie be better contented to yeald accordinglie unto the same. So wee bidd, &c."

Again the outcome of the petition is not known, but one can only assume that it failed, as our rating system today is based on the size of property and land ownership, as opposed to the actual wealth of the person.

In the chapter on St Laurence Church and its

rectors it was noted that the clergy were losing their livings and being replaced by Puritan rectors at the time of the Commonwealth. This had happened at Upminster when John Halke was removed from his living. Just before the end of Cromwell's period as Lord Protector in 1660, John Halke petitioned the Council for his reinstatement. The State Papers for 30th March, 1658, record the events

"The Council heard the petition of John Halke of Upminster Essex sequestered [removed] in 1646 by the Committee of Plundered Ministries for restoration to the liberty of preaching, referred to by the Protector to Council, referred to Nye, Caryll and Peters to consider his certificate and enquire into his fitness to preach and report."

A month later, on 22nd April, a further entry states -

"The report on the petition of John Halke stated he was fit to be restored to the ministry: – order that he be allowed to exercise his gifts whenever he is presented with a living if the Commissioners of Approbation of Public Preachers approve him. Approved 7th May, 1658."

The records show that when Charles II came to the throne Halke got back his rectorship of St Laurence Church.

Gaynes

T L WILSON - UPMINSTER'S HISTORIAN

Thomas Lewis Wilson, although not an educated man, is equally important in Upminster's history as the principal landowners of his time for, although they made the history by their deeds and misdeeds, it was Wilson who had the foresight to record the comings and goings of the village, kept voluminous scrapbooks and also conducted his own historical research.

Thomas Wilson was born in 1833 and died in 1919 at the age of 85. His great-grandfather, Andrew was born in 1753 in Newcastle-upon-Tyne and, although from a working class family, had an aptitude towards learning. Andrew had two sons and one of them, Thomas, moved to Upminster where he earned the reputation of a craftsman and it is reported that he was sadly missed in the village when he died in 1808. Thomas Wilson lived at Tadlows in Corbets Tey Road and died a bachelor. The younger brother, Andrew, undertook his apprenticeship as a carpenter in Newcastle from 1766 to 1773 and, on his move to London, became a staircase maker of some repute. Through his brother he was recommended to Samuel Hammond to superintend the installation of a stair case at Harwood Hall. He worked for Samuel Hammond on various occasions during the latter years of the century before finally taking up residence in the village in 1798 in a cottage in St Mary's Lane, opposite today's school. Andrew Wilson was very well read for an artisan of those days and, like his brother, a year later, his death was mourned by both villagers and gentry alike.

Andrew had four children and Thomas, the second eldest, who was born in 1789, stayed in Upminster, where he worked for Samuel Hammond as a carpenter like his father and, once again, showed intellect above his social standing in the community. Thomas Wilson was the first of the family to record events and the history of the parish and he passed his knowledge and his enthusiasm on to his son, Thomas Lewis Wilson. By 1836, at the age of 47, Thomas Wilson senior worked for himself as a carpenter and undertaker and his son carried on the business after his death in 1875. T L Wilson diversified into builder, brick and tile maker, contractor and renovator of buildings. His builder's yard was in the garden of his father's home in St Mary's Lane, where he now lived. He was in partnership for 30 years with Edward Hook on various building ventures and they held for some time the brickworks in Bird Lane, referred to in Chapter Five.

Wilson's interest in the renovation of property led him into estate agency, although not as we know them today, but merely as an occasional agent for the sale or letting of a property. When the 'Bell' public house was bought by Mr F Seabrook in 1886, he received a commission of £80. It would appear that he was recognised as a principal local businessman, but he did not make his fortune with his various interests, probably because he spent too much time in delving into Upminster's history. He had published two books on Upminster - *Sketches of Upminster* (1856) and *The History and Topography of Upminster* (1880-81); in addition he kept scrapbooks, which in the end ran to 14 volumes, which are now in the Essex Record Office and are available to the public. This book has often referred to Wilson and his published works and for someone who was only educated at a fairly ordinary private school in Hornchurch, his style of writing was very eloquent. In his *Sketches*, published when he was only 23, he describes the surrounding countryside in the first chapter. Referring to the Laindon Hills he says, "As you emerge from a deeply shadowed lane, a magnificent prospect bursts upon the eye, extending in some directions nearly forty miles: an almost boundless valley beneath, painted with the finest verdure, enriched with farms, and studded with mansions, hamlets, villages and woods..."

From Wilson's many scrapbooks only a few sample entries can be reproduced here to show what sort of cuttings and jottings he saw fit to include. He did not just keep cuttings from local newspapers, but used the scrapbook for jottings for his published works on Upminster's history. The first volume, for example, includes

94

Notice of a Court of the Manor of Gaines 1882

Manor of Gaines
in Upminster in Essex

202
Pattison Wigg & Co
11, Queen Victoria St
E.C.

This is to give Notice to all the
Freehold and Copyhold Tenants of the said Manor
That they personally be and appear before me William
King, Gentleman, Steward of the said Manor, at the
Bell Inn at Upminster, upon Thursday the twenty
third day of November, by One of the Clock p.m
of the same day then and there to do their Suit and
service at the General Court Baron of John Jackson,
Esquire, Lord of the said Manor to be then and there
holden for the said Manor

Given under my hand this 20th day
of October in the year of our Lord 1882

William King,

Steward

Essex Record Office

extracts from some of the correspondence that took place between the Lord of the Manor in the 1770s, Sir James Esdaile, Knight, and various people and these letters had all been copied from the original, says Wilson in his comments on these entries. On the first page of the first volume, which was begun in 1881, Wilson writes, "In the following pages there are some 500 extracts, newspaper cuttings and other slips and papers, some of them are locally historic, others novel and quaint, some personally interesting to the present writer or his family, and probably there are some which possess no interest or value whatsoever. They have [been] procured from all sorts of places and if they have only appeared likely to be useful to anyone into whose hands the book might afterwards come it has been sufficient excuse for trying thus to preserve them." Little did Wilson realise, when he wrote those words, how useful his many volumes have been and I hope will be for many generations to come, now that they have been deposited at the Record Office for all to see if they wish.

A typical page of his scrapbook might contain press cuttings about parish business, cuttings regarding happenings to local people, train tickets to Romford [4 old pence] and sometimes signatures of local dignitaries. A few illustrations of and extracts from Wilson's scrapbooks follow. Anyone who is interested in browsing further through these volumes should go to the Essex Record Office where the reference number is T/P 67/ 1-14: prior notice to the Supervisor is essential.

The first item is a notice of a forthcoming general meeting of the Court of the Manor of Gaines in 1882.

The next piece from one of the scrapbooks is an advertisement for Wenn's Stores in The Broadway [Station Road] which presumably was a single sheet either handed out in the shop or pushed through people's doors.

It would seem that the summers a hundred years ago were often no better than we sometimes enjoy today, as there appear a number of press cuttings referring to heavy rainfall and floods during the summer months. This appeared in a local paper on 17th August, 1882 –

FOUND DROWNED IN UPMINSTER

Yesterday an inquest was held at the Bell Inn, Upminster, before Mr C C Lewis upon the body of William Smith,

A CUP OF GOOD TEA.

4/44

A Cup of Wenn's Tea
Is acknowledged to be
A famous restorer in sadness ;
It quicken life's flame,
And enlivens the frame,
And diffuses a spirit of gladness.

When acquaintances meet,
By way of a treat,
In fellowship social and hearty,
A cup of Wenn's Tea
Increases the glee,
And greatly enlivens the party.

When the head is in pain,
And its tenant, the brain,
Seems week in performing its
function,
A cure you may make
If you speedily take
A cup of J. Wenn's famous
unction.

When a lass is in doubt,
And would wish to find out
The real intent of her lover,
Why a cup of Wenn's Tea,
As we oftentimes see,
The secret at once will discover.

If perchance you will send,
To relation or friend,
A cleverly dictated letter,
You have only to try
What this cup will supply—
I assure you, you cannot do
better.

You may roam through the
street,
But you never will meet
With Teas of more exquisite
flavour ;
So give me a call,
And I'll welcome you all,
And return my best thanks for
the favour.

J. WENN,
THE BROADWAY STORES,
UPMINSTER.

Grocery, Drapery, Provision & Italian Goods.

TRY US! PROVE US!! AND RECOMMEND US!!!
FAMILIES WAITED UPON FOR ORDERS.

N 2

aged 58, whose body was found in the Ingrebourne Brook on Tuesday. Eliza Smith said her husband was employed as a labourer by Mr Branfil and the last time she saw him alive was on the morning of the 4th inst. He had not done any work since the previous Tuesday and told her that his master could not find him any on account of the floods. She had had disagreements with him sometimes about the children. About nine years since the deceased was about to take what she believed was poison when he was stopped by his daughter. Henry Wood, a labourer of Hornchurch, spoke of seeing the deceased on Saturday morning, August 4th, at the Harrow Public House when he was quite sober. Deceased accompanied him to London and came back with him the following morning, they breakfasted together at the witness's cottage. They afterwards went out, and he left the deceased at Doggetts Corner, deceased saying he was going home. Deceased was then in his usual spirits and was quite sober. William Hunt said on Sunday morning he was walking by the Ingrebourne Brook and noticed what appeared to be a coat in the water. He could not reach it with a stick and so left it. On Tuesday he again passed the place and on touching the coat with a stick found it to be the body of the deceased. Information given to the police. PC Webb deposed that in company with PC Emery he took the body out of the water. Deceased had apparently been in the water some days. The clothes were not disarranged nor was there any sign of a struggle. A verdict of 'Found Drowned' was returned.

Six years later the *Essex Weekly News* of Friday, 3rd August, 1888, carried the following article –
DISASTROUS STORM AND FLOOD IN ESSEX
Upminster. The Ingrebourne Brook overflowed on Wednesday night the water running over the top of the bridge. The terrific force of the water carried away a long stretch of iron railings outside the Bridge House Inn, cut two long channels along the Hornchurch side of the bridge one of them five feet deep, interrupting vehicular traffic. A number of sheep and pigs were drowned, some belonging to Mr Batson, butcher. The Bridge House Inn was deluged and Mr Lee (the landlord) will suffer serious loss.

98

A further report in the press reads -
Heavy rains of the previous fortnight culminated on the Wednesday night/Thursday morning with an unusually severe and protracted thunderstorm which was accompanied by an incessant and copious downpour lasting upwards of four hours. The accumulation of the overflow from the various watersheds raised the already swollen streams to such a degree that they overflowed their banks and great destruction of property was inevitable.

The report then went on to recall the fate of the various South Essex towns and villages. Romford appears to have suffered the worst with the Ind, Coope brewery estimating their damage at £30,000: the water level was three feet high in the brewery yard and 5/6 feet high in the lower parts of the brewery ground. All the villages south of Chelmsford down to the river from Stanford-le-Hope to Barking were also affected by serious flooding.

Wilson wrote a letter to the *Essex Times* published in their edition of 29th March, 1890, probably prompted by the flooding of recent years. He wrote regarding the need for a drainage scheme for the village and alluded to the many complaints heard as to the defective way in which the village was drained at the present. The London, Tilbury & Southend Railway had just started their new line from Upminster to Grays and Wilson suggested the company might lay a sewer at the same time, which could be connected into the village system. Apparently nothing came of this suggestion at the time.

The following extract is from the *Essex Weekly News* of 29th August, 1890, and is included in Wilson's scrapbooks for that year -
Messrs Turner, Haynes and Clifton applied on behalf of Ind Coope & Co. Ltd. for a full licence for premises to be built on a site in Hall Lane within 160 yards of Upminster Railway Station. They submitted plans which they said showed that ample accommodation was to be provided. There was no desire to interfere with the trade of the Bell, which was an old fashioned house doing a very satisfactory trade. The intention was to provide accommodation for passengers to and from Upminster Station. Twenty six trains a day passed the station daily with occasional "specials" and at these times the accommodation at the Bell was totally inadequate. Upminster

would shortly become an important junction as the railway to Grays and the docks was nearing completion... Mr
Maitland on behalf of the freeholder of the Bell said that
the application would mean starvation to both houses.
Messrs Ind Coope & Co. Ltd. had a lease on the Bell
which had 9 years yet to run. They had an opportunity a
few months since to acquire the freehold, but they did
not do so and they were now looking forward to getting a
licenced house without the expense of buying a freehold.
The Chairman of the Petty Sessions, which were being
heard at Brentwood, refused the application.

There is also reference in Wilson's scrapbooks to
an earlier application in July, 1888, also by Ind Coope for
a licence for a public house. This previous application was
also dismissed, but the description of the site is more
definite than in 1890. The earlier application pinpointed
the site as exactly where the 'Essex Yeoman' stands
today!

The following press cutting in the scrapbooks is
dated 1882 -

CHARGE OF ROBBING TILL AT UPMINSTER

On Thursday, at the Court House, Brentwood, Thomas
Freeman, a labourer of Rainham, was charged before
Major Newton with stealing on Tuesday a sum of money
from the till of the Hacton White Hart, Upminster
belonging to Mr William Cracknell, the landlord. Emma
Cracknell, wife of prosecutor, stated that about one
o'clock on Tuesday, the prisoner entered her tap room
with two other men named Cook and Cressy and called
for two pots of beer. Witness was in the bar when they
entered, and prisoner came there to fetch the beer and
carried it back to the tap room. After a few minutes
witness left the bar and there was then a basin containing silver standing in the till which was closed. In about
three minutes she heard some money rattle and at once
went into the bar and found the basin upset and the
prisoner walking away from the tap room. She accused
him of taking some money; she then saw him take some
silver from his trousers pocket. As he was leaving the
house she put her hand in his pocket and pulled out half
a crown which she found to be one she had marked with
lead pencil. Major Newton - Why did you mark the piece
of money? - So that the men there should not cheat me;

they very often tender me a florin and upon receiving their change say it was half a crown. The prisoner came back in about two minutes and asked her for the half a crown and she told him the policeman would give it to him. She believed that about 15 shillings had been taken from the till. P.C.Boreham, stationed at Upminster, deposed to apprehending the prisoner at Rainham, and when he charged him the prisoner said, "I did not have it". It wa about half past nine in the evening. Prisoner was then remanded till next Thursday.

There is no further record as to the outcome of the case.

Wilson, in his capacity as a land agent in a small way, was concerned when the lease of New Place came up for sale in 1874, when the following appeared in the local paper -

LEASE TO BE SOLD (three miles from Romford Station), a capital FAMILY RESIDENCE prettily situate in the village of Upminster, Essex, standing high and commanding a good view. It is approached by a carriage drive and comprises 12 bed rooms, dressing rooms, nursery, etc., drawing room 35ft by 25ft, dining room, library, ante room and good offices: stabling for six horses, coach houses, coachman's room and premises, gardener's cottage and farm yard, large gardens, lawns and conservatories, vineries, ornamental piece of water affording fishing and boating; plantation walk to church, wherein are pews in right of house; 38 acres of productive meadow land, which reduces the rent of £238 to about £100 per annum. The lease has 17 years to run and is to be sold. Four packs of hounds within a short distance. Apply to Mr. Wilson, builder, Upminster.

Also in the same year there was a fire at New Place and, once again, Wilson was involved - this time as builder and part-time fireman. The cost of restoration Wilson notes alongside the press cutting was £23.

FIRE - On Monday, October 22nd, a fire which, if it had not been promptly subdued, would in all probability have turned out to be a very serious matter, occurred in the extensive range of stabling at the residence of Mr Laurie, New Place, Upminster. It appears that on Sunday the coachman applied a match to a curtain, where a gas pipe was leaking, and did not effectually extinguish it. The consequence was that on the following morning the fire broke out in the roof in a very alarming manner. Mr Wilson, builder, of Upminster, who was immediately summoned by Mr Laurie, set to work, and with the aid of several men soon stripped the roof and put out the fire. The damage, which is not very serious, is covered by Insurance in the County Fire Office.

It was mentioned that Wilson was in partnership with Edward Hook as a brick and tile maker at the brick-fields in Bird Lane in the 1880s. An advertisement of those times reads -

BEST RED BRICKS

PIPES, TILES AND POTTERY

BUILDING BRICKS	SOCKET PIPES
PAVING BRICKS	DRAIN PIPES
FRENCH TILES	FLOWER POTS
PAN TILES	CHIMNEY POTS
PLAIN TILES KALE POTS, SEED PANS	

ORNAMENTAL BRICKS AND TILES TO ORDER

WILSON AND HOOK, UPMINSTER

Finally, in this extract of Wilson's activities he can be seen as a part-time employment agency, when he advertises on behalf of a friend or possibly an illiterate farm employee the following -
SITUATION WANTED, as STEWARD or FARM BAILIFF
in a small place of trust; 26 years character;
the strongest and highest recommendations from
Sir T.B.Lennard, Bart., Belhus, Aveley, and
from Henry Joslin Esq., J.P., Gaines Park,
Upminster. - Apply to Mr.T.L.Wilson, Builder,
Upminster.

It is hoped that these few extracts will whet your appetite to delve further into the Wilson scrapbooks at Chelmsford.

As well as being an historian and recording the words and deeds of others, he was a forward thinking man and recognised as such in the community. He had the bright idea of sealing some objects into the rebuilt bridge over the River Ingrebourne at Upminster Bridge. A special receptacle was prepared into which was placed a copy of Wilson's *History and Topography of Upminster*, including on the fly-leaf autographs of many local residents. Also enclosed were copies of local newspapers, coins, photographs and a number of documents of general interest. The contents were sealed up on 9th December, 1891 into the centre of the east wall on the Upminster bank of the Ingrebourne, seven feet below the road surface.

Wilson's popularity in the village was shown when the Upminster Parish Council was first formed in 1894 and he became a Councillor, which post he held until 1902. At the first election in 1894 Wilson polled 87 votes out of a total of 1,175, spread over 17 candidates - of which he came fifth. The highest number of votes cast for any one candidate was 103 for Isaac Gay, the farmer of Great Sunnings, Corbets Tey. Wilson held various local offices, but it was probably his contribution and, in particular, his evidence to a Parliamentary enquiry for which he should be best remembered.

The Romford to Grays railway line was to be constructed (the Fenchurch Street-Upminster-Southend line being already in existence) and the proposed route from Romford was for the line to cross the Hornchurch Road at Wingletye Lane and thence to Corbets Tey, by-passing Upminster altogether. Wilson's strong evidence to the enquiry in favour of the line coming through Upminster must have had the desired effect for the route was subsequently changed.

Thomas Lewis Wilson will be remembered, not only for his contribution to the community as an administrator and public figure, but also, and principally, for his great contribution to the collecting, recording and publishing of Upminster's history up to the latter part of the 19th century, which continued thereafter in his scrapbooks until his death in 1919. Upminster is in the enviable position of having had T L Wilson as a resident, for, although there are sources that would enable most communities to write their own history today, Wilson started collecting his information and talking to residents well over a hundred years ago, which has given Upminster a head start and consequently events and facts have been recorded that would otherwise have been lost and gone forever.

T L Wilson

VESTRY AND PARISH BUSINESS

The administration of a village in medieval times was conducted by the Lord of the Manor through what was called the Courts Baron and, in Upminster's case, there are records dating back to 1607 of meetings at Upminster Hall. The Court, however, would probably have been formally established in the 13th century. For Gaynes Manor no medieval records have been found, but there are papers of meetings of the Court Baron from 1678 to 1923.

In medieval times the Lords of the Manors usually owned the whole village and it followed that all the administration was centred round the Lord's own Court. As these large estates were slowly broken up and a village acquired residents who owned their own land, a form of local government was set up covering the whole village, whilst the Manor Court dealt with matters concerning only the land belonging to the Lord of the Manor and the people residing thereon.

Records for the Parish of Upminster survive from 1681 and these, together with other parish records, are all deposited at the Essex Record Office. The meetings were held in the vestry of St Laurence Church and parish business in these early days was called Vestry business. The members of the Vestry were duly elected by the inhabitants. The Rector appears to always have been a member of the Vestry and, in 1799 for example, other officers were one churchwarden appointed by the rector, one churchwarden appointed by the parish, an overseer for the poor for each of the North and South wards, a constable and a vestry clerk. As one might imagine, the vestry was a very chilly venue for a meeting in the winter and in the minutes for 4th February, 1799, they relate the following halfway through the agenda –

"... We, the undersigned, being the Officers of this

Parish who have met at the church to settle last month's accounts, having gone through part of the business do unanimously agree to adjourn this Vestry to the Bell, the inclemency of the weather making it hardly possible to transact the whole here..."

Obviously it was warmer in the public house, where it is sure that rum and whisky were available to thaw the body. It is noticeable that meetings were thereafter either adjourned or held at the 'Bell' on many occasions. Incidentally, the landlord of the 'Bell' at this time was Joseph Lee, who was an overseer of the poor and therefore a parish officer. It was probably his suggestion that took the meeting across the road to his hostelry.

The main responsibilities of the Vestry were the maintenance of the church, the roads and bridges and the wellbeing and upkeep of the poor. Reports and Accounts had to be submitted regularly to the County Quarter Sessions and a summons could be issued if these were not delivered on time. The time the Vestry spent on the poor of the village was far in excess of that on other matters and due credit must go to the eminent parishioners of those days for being such responsible people in ensuring that the poor were cared for. Records dating back to the 16th century show that, even then, Upminster had a responsibility for the poor as, in 1567, a poor box was in evidence in the church. From then, until the mid-18th century, the poor were lodged by the Vestry in local cottages for an agreed sum. In 1740 the parish was paying for about 18 people to lodge in the village at a rental of 30 shillings [£1.50] a year. Besides paying rent, the Vestry authorised payments to the villagers for the upkeep of the poor in their care at the rate of a few shillings a week. To recoup this expenditure the Vestry had authority to levy rates for the upkeep of the poor and to appoint two officers to look after them. By the mid-18th century the poor of Upminster were becoming a drain on the parish finances and by this time many parishes had established a Workhouse under the Act of 1722. Incidentally, Hornchurch had built their's as early as 1720 and it was now time for Upminster to do the same. For the Workhouse's story see page 20.

Life in the workhouse was hard and pauper burials of all ages were commonplace. Paupers were always buried on the north side of the churchyard in a place away from other graves. Despite improvements in work-houses generally, with the introduction of visiting doctors, hospital treatment, education and visits by Parish Officers, the early 19th century was a difficult time and the depression that was affecting the country must have been felt in the standard of living at Upminster's workhouse. Unemployment was high and, once again, the cost of main-taining the workhouse was a drain on the Vestry's income. The rates charged to the residents were always increasing and there was discontent at the cost of main-taining the paupers. When the responsibility was trans-ferred to Romford in 1836 the Vestry must have breathed a sigh of relief.

The Vestry minutes give a good insight into the problems faced in connection with the poor, the sick and the needy and also those that just passed through the parish. An Act of 1697 allowed a poor person to enter another parish, provided he had a certificate from his own parish and was also distinguished by the letter 'P' on his right sleeve, followed the the first letter of his own parish. Upminster's poor therefore bore the letters 'PU', whereas in Hornchurch the letters were 'PH'. The poor were not keen to wear this obvious stigma and the Vestry officers were empowered not to pass over Poor Relief to those not wearing their letters. In 1749 the Vestry minutes indicate that the sleeve lettering had been re-placed by a 'PU' badge.

Parishioners tended to live the best part of their lives in their own parish and seldom ventured away. The average villager did not have the ability to travel, anyway, as a horse and cart would have been the most they would have owned. Consequently if a poor family came to Upminster it was the duty of the Overseer to enquire their whereabouts and to obtain the acknowledgement of their own parish that, although they were currently residing in Upminster, they were still responsible for them and to pay them poor relief if necessary. Conversely, Upminster was responsible for its own poor if they were residing in another parish. The Vestry minutes make various references to money being sent all over Essex to parishes where Upminster's poor were temporarily resident. This operation was costly both in monetary terms and also in the administration of sending money elsewhere and occasionally the Vestry considered bringing the person or family back to Upminster.

In 1710 John Buggy and his wife, Francis, were brought back from Thaxted. Later in the 18th century, William Mann, the Overseer, records the problems of the Crowest family: Crowest was a native of Leeds, Kent, but living in Upminster and not married to the mother of his children. The parish decided to send him back to Leeds, but Crowest heard of the plans and ran away, to be followed by the Overseer. The trail led to Stifford and then Burstead before Crowest was apprehended. The Overseer then claimed expenses for four days to get the family back to Kent. Unfortunately the Vestry of Leeds sent the family back again and it appears that when the family returned to Upminster Charles Crowest finally married, the Vestry paying for the wedding, which cost them £2.6.0d [£2.30]. Apparently Crowest then left the parish and the family were supported by the Vestry as various entries record. Possibly he only married her to ensure that they would be looked after when he moved on. One of the descendants of the family eventually made good, for Thomas Crowest became Vestry Clerk for 1831-34 and also Master of the Parochial School. He also wrote the first history of the parish in 1830.

The health of the poor was also a parish responsibility and, in an early case, Dr George Aylett of Romford agreed with Hornchurch parish for a set sum to cure the leg of one, Jonas Durham. When the bill was submitted to Hornchurch the parish contended that Durham was an Upminster resident and that they should settle the account. A legal battle ensued and the case ended up at the Brentwood Assizes, with the parties eventually going to arbitration, allowing one prominent resident of each parish to get together to settle the matter. Unfortunately for both parishes the bill and legal costs ended up at £30, which was a great deal of money in those days. It is uncertain who paid the bill or whether it was divided equally.

The poor children of the parish had to be found work and this was the responsibility of the Overseer of the Poor. Upminster being a rural parish meant that boys went to local farmers and girls into large houses as servants. Up till 1766 boys were 'apprenticed' until the age of 24, but this was reduced that year to the age of 21. Girls were apprenticed until they reached 21 or when they married, if this was sooner.

The parish records show that Upminster was caring for its poor that became sick and there are many references to money being spent on medicines, liniments and lotions. The parish also sent the poor to hospital if they thought this would be beneficial and, in 1811, Eleanor Hummerson was admitted to St Bartholomew's Hospital with 'sickness and lameness', with a promise that the parish would receive her back 'when discharged from hospital or to bury her if she dies there'. The bill was duly received that Eleanor spent 147 days in hospital at a cost of £3.13.6d, the parish having sent on admission £1.15.0d. It would seem that she stayed in hospital a lot longer than the parish anticipated.

In the 18th century the poor were paid a weekly allowance by the parish of between five and seventeen pence, although it was always cheaper for the parish if residents gave them cast-off clothing, etc. During the winter the poor were given coal and faggots and it was not unknown for a labourer to be given a particular tool to enable him to earn his living better. A common complaint among the poor was the one referred to as the 'itch', which, although uncomfortable, was only a minor complaint, while the feared illness of the 18th century was smallpox. Wine and gin were often given to seriously ill people and beer to those convalescing.

The insane occasionally featured in the Overseer's accounts and, in 1737, one, John Perry, had to be restrained by soldiers brought into the parish, which proved expensive as a beer allowance was paid to the soldiers that appeared to be increasing with every entry in the records. Eventually the parish decided to get Perry admitted to Bethlehem Royal Hospital (Bedlam) in Finsbury Square which cost the parish 10/- [50p] in transportation and nearly £4 in admission charges.

The Vestry was responsible overnight for poor people passing through Upminster en route for some other parish, provided they produced a pass from the parish from whence they came, stating where they were going. They would be given a night's lodging and food and then sent on their way. In 1816 George and Elizabeth Turner were apprehended in Northampton for begging and, when it was discovered they came from Upminster, they were sent from parish to parish via the local constables to enable them to get food and lodgings, until they reached Upminster when they were delivered to the Overseer of the Poor.

Another category of casual poor were the families of soldiers who had gone to the wars in France in the 1790s, and who were being returned home following a change of policy. The unfortunate families were dumped at Tilbury and told to find their way home. Consequently, many people passed through Upminster with poor passes issued by the Army, en route to as far flung places as Yorkshire and Wales.

Having cared for the poor all their lives, the parish was responsible for burying them. This also included those poor parishioners who died outside the parish and had to be brought back to Upminster at the parish's expense. When Richard Rowell died in 1796 'on the King's highway by the inclemency of the weather', it resulted in the parish paying for the funeral and then, unfortunately, having to transport Widow Rowell to the workhouse with her belongings.

Whilst in the workhouse the Vestry had to administer medical attention when necessary and it is clear that the majority of those people attending to Upminster's poor were not doctors, but quacks and herbalists. It was not until 1764 that the parish decided to have a contract with a doctor and the Vestry minutes of 1767 record the arrangement for that particular year –

"It is agreed by the Parish of Upminster this day met in Vestry and Francis Bernard of Hornchurch that in consideration of the said Francis Bernard attending and supplying the Poor taking Alms and residing and belonging to the said Parish of Upminster or elsewhere not exceeding two miles from Upminster Church; the smallpox and broken bones excepted. And that the Overseers of the said Parish of Upminster shall pay the said Francis Bernard the sum of £5.5.0 per annum half yearly to commence the Tuesday Vestry in Easter last part."

Notwithstanding the parish having a contract with one doctor, they still used others on a casual basis. By

1801 Dr Thomas London had come to live in Upminster. Previously he had had a contract with the parish since 1791 and that for 1797 records a fee of £12.12.0d.

"Agreement made this day in Vestry between the Churchwardens and Overseers of the Parish of Upminster and Thomas London, Apothecary of Upminster, for and in consideration of the sum of £12.12.0 to him annually paid convenants daily to attend the poor belonging to the said parish in all cases where medical or sugical assistance is required whether such poor persons are resident therein or in any of the neighbouring parishes herein specified as Romford, Hornchurch, Cranham, Laindon, Aveley and North Ockendon, finding the medicines required upon application made to him by such persons who shall produce an order signed by some officer of the said parish or their clerk, and also to attend any of the said poor as a midwife where a woman who is such cannot do the business. This agreement to continue in force for three years from the date thereof."

The parish was divided into two wards, North and South, the dividing line being the road from Hornchurch to Cranham (St Mary's Lane). For each ward there was appointed a churchwarden, an overseer of the poor, a surveyor responsible for highways and bridges and a constable. At the start of the chapter it was said that the rector appointed one warden and this was the case right up to the eighteen hundreds. For the position of Overseer of the Poor the Vestry appointed one for each ward up to 1733, but thereafter the Justices selected the two from nominations put forward by the Vestry. Similarly, around this time, the Justices appointed the highway surveyors and constables. The Vestry Clerk was a salaried position and record of this dates back as far as 1701. In the 1740s the parish appointed a dog whipper, who was later called the Beadle and, after that, the Sexton.

As previously mentioned, the Parish rate had always been a matter of some concern to the inhabitants and especially the amount collected for poor relief, which was a great drain on the parish coffers. About 1710 two-thirds of the rates collected went towards the upkeep of the poor; by 1800 the proportion had risen to five sixths; and in 1810 all the rates that year went towards the poor.

In 1799 there were still problems with the inequalities of the general rate system and so the Vestry appointed two qualified surveyors to survey and value the whole parish. The fee was agreed at four pence an acre for land and £1.50 per acre for property.

With the closing of the workhouse in 1836 and transferring the inmates to Romford the parish was thankful for the burden being taken from its shoulders, but rates still had to be collected for the poor, but, other than passing the money over, there were no further responsibilities and so the work of the Vestry was greatly reduced. It seems that interest in the business of the parish waned as soon as the time consuming problems of the poor had been taken away from the parish. In 1836 the Vestry Clerk was Jesse Oxley, who was also appointed Assistant Overseer and Surveyor of the highways. He probably took on these extra jobs as nobody else would.

The Essex Constabulary had been formed in 1843, but the parish was still appointing its own Constable in 1866. The Local Government Act was passed in 1894 and the parish was obliged to form a Parish Council: this is the start of local government as we know it today and it sees the end of the parish committee, the Vestry, and an elected Council in its stead.

Upminster's first election took place at the end of 1894 with 17 candidates standing for the 9 places on the new Upminster Parish Council. The candidates and the votes cast were -

John Arkell Abraham	67	votes	James Noader	47	
Ernest James Brown	88	*	Edward Pearman	45	
Alfred Morgan Carter	94	*	Frank Herbert Rowe	101	*
Richard Clark	83	*	Lewis Oxley Rowe	63	
William Cook	40		George Frederick West	79	*
Henry Dearing	69	*	Thomas Lewis Wilson	87	*
Isaac Mathew Gay	103	*	Edwin Sydney Woodwin	89	*
Matthew Johnson	22				
Henry Joslin	56				
Joseph Frances Leslier	42		Those elected marked *		

In 1894 the population was about 1,450, with about 350 allowed to vote. The electorate had more than one vote and it is estimated that about 250 people did so. The initial enthusiasm of electing the Parish Council soon

waned, for, whereas in the first election 69 votes secured
the ninth seat, in the following year just 18 votes elected
a candidate. Voting increased in subsequent years, but by
1901 there was no election, due to the lack of nominations. Despite the apathy of the electorate those repres-
enting the parish excelled in their duties and those early
councillors are owed a debt for shaping the village which
was fast becoming a rural suburb of London.

The gradual increase in the population to nearly
1,500 had meant that the churchyard was becoming full
and one of the first problems for the new Council was
the provision of further ground for burials. A sub-
committee was set up in 1895 to consider ways of
acquiring more land. This committee co-opted the assistance of the Trustees of the Branfils of Upminster Hall
and several sites were put forward. These were on
Upminster Hill, near the windmill; on Barksey Downs to
the southeast of Hall Lane; and a site behind New Place,
towards Corbets Tey Road. The Trustees were not
enamoured with any of these sites suggested by the
Council, but they offered only one site, well away from
the centre of the village towards Cranham. There being
no agreement with the Trustees, on whose land the
cemetery would be built, the matter was dropped for two
years, when the Parish Council passed a resolution
recommending that the Rector be approached for a
portion of the Glebe to be purchased as a cemetery.
Later the same year the Council went to the other large
landowner, Henry Joslin of Gaynes Manor, to purchase
land adjacent to Tadlows. This also fell through. Finally,
in December, 1898, Western & Sons offered the Parish $2\frac{1}{2}$
acres of land in Corbets Tey for £450 for the purpose of
a cemetery. Of the nine Councillors, four abstained from
the vote and the motion to acquire was passed with three
Councillors voting in favour. The capital sum needed to
buy the land and develop the site was £2,500, which was
borrowed. The site was dedicated on 9th May, 1902, and
it was, of course, the original cemetery grounds in
Corbets Tey, next to which the crematorium has now
been built.

With the coming of the railway to Upminster in
1885, it was clear that the population would soon grow,
although the development of the village did not really

begin until 1900. Nevertheless, during the 19th century the population had doubled from 765 in 1801 and consequently Upminster's drainage was failing to cope with the extra people living in the village. Miss Rigby, who lived at Hacton House, but also owned West Lodge in Corbets Tey Road, complained to the Council in 1895 that she could not find a tenant for West Lodge due to the state of the drainage ditch, which was no better than an open sewer. In 1896 the resident of Holly Lodge, opposite the Rectory, also complained to the Council about the smell from the ditch in front of his house. Various proposals were put forward to buy land for a drainage scheme, but each time the residents local to the land in question objected. Finally, in 1899, five acres of land on Henry Joslin's Gaynes estate were bought. The site was in the vicinity of the River Ingrebourne roughly where the Hornchurch Stadium car park is today. The cost was £515 for the site and for the construction of a sewage plant a further £4,401, which was sanctioned by the Local Government Board.

An interesting snippet from the Council minutes refers to the ford across the Ingrebourne at Upminster Bridge, which was south of the existing bridge, where the squash club entrance is located. Apparently the land on the Upminster side of the approach was in a neglected state and the Council proposed that Essex County Council's attention be drawn to it before someone enclosed it and this area was lost to the parish. This piece of land, albeit only wide enough for a carriage, was owned, along with the road over the bridge, by the County Council. The County took no action and by 1909 someone had encroached on this strip of land. The County raised no objections, as obviously the piece of land was of no use to them. Land was very cheap in those days, but one cannot see that sort of thing happening today without the powers that be intervening!

By 1911 Upminster's population had risen to 2,468 and, in 1913, the Council was authorised to have 12 members, an increase of 3. Meetings were held in one of the schools and gradually the feeling was that Upminster should have its own Council offices. The Council advertised in local papers in 1915 for land suitable for such a building, which proved to be an unpopular move. Many people had moved from London to Upminster for a reduction in rates and, of course, a municipal building would be expensive to run. The residents saw no reason why the parish council, with its limited powers, should not continue its meetings in school premises. Many letters appeared in the local press against the idea of a Town Hall, as it was now being called, except for one correspondent who suggested purchasing the Clock House, the old stable block of New Place recently purchased by W P Griggs. With the Great War now a major preoccupation little was then heard of a Town Hall until 1922 when the Council resurrected the idea. This time there were no objections from the ratepayers and the Clock House was looked at as a possible site. Housing development was now in full swing and the original plan was to pull New Place and its adjoining Clock House stable block down for building development. The Council put forward two schemes to the parish, one just to buy the Clock House and limited ground for £1,800 or, alternatively, to buy both buildings and a little land for £3,000. The voting was

	For	Against
For buying the Clock House	153	151
For buying New Place, etc	81	155

Thus, by a margin of two votes, the electorate decided in favour of the cheaper scheme. In April, 1924, Essex County Council confirmed the purchase and a loan of £2,000 was raised to cover the transaction and conversion costs. The foresight of the parish councillors in preserving this part of the New Place estate from building developers can still be seen, with its impressive clock tower.

The 1920s saw housing development eating up the available land around the village centre and the old buildings, like New Place, were gradually disappearing. Once again, the timely action of the parish council saved a central area from housing development – this time the campaign was for a recreation ground. Councillor Key submitted a scheme in September, 1920, whereby the Glebe, owned by the church, should be acquired for this purpose. A public meeting was called in November and the resolution that the Council should purchase $12\frac{3}{4}$ acres of the Glebe for not more than £3,759 was debated. The land was to be used as a recreation ground, with the proviso that 200 feet of the frontage be reserved for special buildings, such as Council Offices or some other community building. An amendment was proposed at the meeting that, while appreciating the Council's laudable motives, the ratepayers could not consent to acquiring the land for such a purpose in view of the expense and lack of future income. A vote was taken with 16 parishioners in favour of the Council's scheme and 31 in favour of the amendment to turn the proposition aside. There the matter was left for some years and it was generally expected that the land, like other central plots, would be sold for housing. The matter came up again in 1927 when negotiations were well in hand for the Glebe to be sold to the Upminster Sports and Social Club who were already using it for sporting activities. By the June of 1927 the purchase price had been agreed and the Council had approved the plans for diverting the footpaths that criss-crossed the Glebe so that they would not interfere with the facilities. This scheme fell through and this was the opportunity for the Parish Council to ressurect its own plans to buy the land. The Council approached the Rector, who, in turn, asked the Church Commissioners, and finally in March, 1929, a scheme was agreed whereby the consideration was to be £6,000 payable over a period of 70 years. The agreement was, once again, for a piece of the frontage to be earmarked for municipal buildings, from which the parish hoped to get £100 a year from lettings. The parishioners voted again, some 9 years after their initial refusal to buy, and this time were unanimously for the resolution with 130 voters in attendance.

Having acquired the land and converted it into a recreation ground the whole parish was then enthusiastic about the project and decided to plant trees around the perimeter. Subscription lists were drawn up and the sum of £8.10.6d was collected. This sum purchased 51 trees, with the Ratepayers' Association donating two fir trees. The trees and their planting positions were –
South side, along Corbets Tey Road: 5 scarlet thorn, 5 acacia, 5 mountain ash; 5 flowering cherry.
East side, along St Mary's Lane: 5 Canadian poplar, 3 birch, 2 white chestnut.
By the north gates (St Mary's Lane): 5 silver birch, 5

flowering almond, 5 purple plum.
By the west gates (Corbets Tey Road): 2 red chestnut, 2 limes, 2 beech. Not many of those 53 trees remain today.

Upminster Parish Council had very limited powers and most of the important decisions, especially those involving expense, had to be channelled through the Essex County Council. In the early 1900s Upminster's population had grown considerably and much is due to the Parish Council and the local developers in the way they promoted the village as a new Garden Suburb. Hornchurch had previously not been regarded as any great competition to Upminster as a place to live, but, whereas in the early days of growth Upminster's new property was considered better than that of Hornchurch it became clear that Hornchurch, with its development of large estates of average priced housing, was quickly overtaking Upminster. This falling behind in terms of total population was a disappointment to the parish council for, even in 1911, the Council was discussing applying to the Essex County Council for self-government as an Urban District Council. At a council meeting in that year it was decided that no action be taken at the present time to apply for Urban status.

In 1919 the subject was raised again, when it was noticed that Hornchurch was preparing their application. This time it was the Ratepayers' Association who brought the matter to the Council, but once again it was decided that the time was not yet ripe. In 1911 Upminster's population had been 2,468 and by 1919 it was only about 3,500, while Hornchurch now had over 10,000 people.

Five years later, in 1924, correspondence in the *Romford Recorder* referred to other local parishes moving forward with their applications and it was felt that Upminster was dragging its feet. Both Hornchurch and Dagenham attained Urban District status in 1926, leaving Upminster, Cranham and Great Warley as parishes. The following year saw Cranham approach Upminster with a view to a joint application, but Upminster's council turned the idea aside. Although the council had rejected this marriage Upminster's council was now very much aware of what was happening around it and took note of the County's Local Government Committee's comment that it was not prepared to agree to Urban status if a

group of parishes did not meet the population requirements. Any chance of a joint application from Upminster
and Cranham was dashed when it was seen that West
Thurrock and Aveley's joint application was rejected.

There the matter rested until 1929 when a
resolution was passed in council supporting an application
for Urban status jointly by Upminster, Cranham, Great
Warley, Rainham and Wennington. The application was
duly lodged and all seemed to be going well until
Upminster were advised of a dramatic development. Notwithstanding the joint application already on the table at
County Hall, Hornchurch, who obviously knew of the
application, lodged a counter-petition to annex Upminster
and Cranham into their Urban District. It would seem
that there was no love lost between Upminster and Hornchurch and the former's council passed the expected
resolution that the annexing was not acceptable to either
Upminster or Cranham. An invitation had been sent by
Hornchurch to discuss the matter, but Upminster replied,
saying that the invitation was declined as an application
for Urban status was already with the county authorities.

This stalemate situation dragged on for two more
years until February, 1931, when it was recommended
that the five parishes named in the joint application
petition the County by sending personal representatives.
Rainham and Wennington declined to send a councillor and
it appeared from the general apathy that everyone was
resigned that the joint application would be turned down
and that Hornchurch's counter-proposal would win the
day. The inevitable was not finally announced until May,
1933, when it was decided that Upminster and Cranham
parishes were to form part of Hornchurch Urban District,
which was also to include parts of Ockendon, Harold
Wood and Warley, together with the former parishes of
Rainham and Wennington. These new additions were to be
represented by 8 Councillors, whereas Hornchurch and
Emerson Park would have 13 members. It was clear that
future policy would be controlled by the Hornchurch block
of councillors, which was equable in that Hornchurch's
population had risen to 28,000, while Upminster parish
was only about 6,000 and the other new parishes brought
into the District Council did not exceed Hornchurch's
total population.

The last meeting of the Upminster Parish Council was on Wednesday, 21st March, 1934, when all the committee were thanked for their work, especially the Clerk to the Council, who had served the parish faithfully for the previous 25 years.

From then onwards Upminster's parish business was no more and anything relevant to Upminster was dealt with by representatives on the HUDC. In 1965 Hornchurch and Romford merged into the London Borough of Havering.

Upminster Parish.

COUNCIL OFFICES,
ST. MARY'S LANE,
UPMINSTER,
ROMFORD, ESSEX,

Reference
James Crowest

Official Communications should be addressed impersonally to "The Clerk of the Council," or "Assistant Overseer," as the case may be.

Feb 1st 1926

Revd Sir,

Would you let me know whether there is in the Church Registers a person of the name of James Crowest, born about 1825 ? Also the charge for searching the Registers.

Yours faithfully,

A.V.Rieback

Assistant Overseer

The Revd
H.H.Holden
    Upminster
    Rectory.

CRIME AND PUNISHMENT

It is not until Elizabeth times that records are available of crimes and their punishment in the parish of Upminster. Records for the two manors of Gaynes and Upminster Hall do not exist before 1607 and, although in Elizabethan times the manor courts controlled the majority of the village, these courts declined with the establishment of parish committees – the Vestry. Consequently little can be gleaned from the manor courts of misdeeds in the village and the major sources of reference are the Essex Quarter Session records, which are available from 1566, the records of the Archdeacon's Court, the Parish Vestry and local historians of the time, like T L Wilson.

Before recounting some of the crimes that have taken place in the village, it is pertinent to explain the workings of the Archdeacon's Court. As its name suggests it was a court administered by the church and the majority of cases brought before it was of a non-criminal nature, but not necessarily connected with those who obtained their living from the church. Any villager could be summoned to appear before the court if the crime in some way was not in keeping with the standards expected of the villagers in their everyday life. For example, villagers were brought to the Archdeacon's Court for non-appearance in church, for working on Sunday, or even for attending a church other than their own.

Although detailed records of crime in Upminster do not commmence until the 16th century, there is reference to wholesale stealing in Upminster in 1267 by a certain Richard de Southchurch, who came from the Southend area. This incident, as well as many others in south Essex, happened when Henry III (1216-72) was engaged in the second Barons' War and there was general confusion in the country. Richard de Southchurch requisitioned much food and goods in south Essex, making out that they were wanted for the King. The records show that from Thomas of Newland, William of Diss and the clergy of Upminster he took cattle, chickens, hams, carcasses and military stores. In Ockendon he took 8 cocks and many chickens and in every village he visited many eggs to make poultices for the wounded. He always said that the items taken were for the King to help in his wars against the Barons, but the goods were all taken to his house in Southchurch. He was imprisoned in 1285 for other offences and fined £1,000 four years later, although he redeemed the fine by passing to the King his manor at Hatfield Peverel. Richard died in 1294, but it is unlikely that Upminster, or any of the other villages pillaged, ever had their goods returned or reimbursed.

Our licensing laws today are strict, but as early as 1495 an Act was passed empowering local magistrates to allow the selling of ale only where they thought fit. A further Act was passed in 1551/2 reinforcing the law that nobody should keep an alehouse without permission of the justices. The villagers of those times were hard drinkers and consequently enterprising locals started up alehouses without the necessary licence – most probably in their own houses. The Quarter Sessions of 1602 records that Diggory Smart of Upminster had victualled without a licence for five months "in a very unconvenient place". In the same year Richard Rowbothan was presented to the Court for victualling for three months without a licence. In 1613 Thomas Whatman of Upminster, a tailor, was charged with keeping a victualling house without a licence, allowing much disorder in his house, with being drunk and being a profaner of the Sabbath by drinking during the time of prayer. Five villagers, John Browne, Henry Turner, Richard Freeman, John Poulter and Joan Tomson, were brought to court in 1632 for "disordering of themselves by drinking, fighting and quarrelling on a Sunday at the time of Divine Service in the month of September last".

The Quarter Session records of 1642 give an insight into life in the village as far as the more humble villager was concerned. It can be seen that unlicenced alehouses abounded and the records show that Widow Lowdam of Upminster brought much trouble on herself by operating an unlicenced house. Widow Lowdam was the relict of

Stephen Lowdam, who died in 1641 and was possibly landlord of the 'Bell' Inn. She was refused a licence after his
death and probably continued selling ale at the 'Bell'
nevertheless. Unfortunately, even those who supplied beer
to unlicenced premises were contravening the law and
John Lucas of Brentwood, beerbrewer, was presented at
the Quarter Sessions for selling and delivering to Mary
Lowdam of Upminster 40 barrels of strong beer, she not
having a licence. The villagers were obviously very upset
with the conduct of Mary Lowdam and also with a
certain Fred Sweeting who the parishioners themselves
petitioned the Court, through Rector John Halke –
Quarter Sessions, Volume 21, 316/89.

"Petition of the parishioners of Upminster showing the
great abuse and high disorder that are committed in two
alehouses, at Fred Sweeting's and Widow Luddum's
[Lowdam] upon which disorders request was made to the
Justices at the Petty Sessions for the suppression of
them... But yet they refuse to obey the order made and
do yet sell beer without licence. The disorders are very
great; they will suffer men to sit drinking or gaming or
both two days and a night together and not make them
depart, but are content with such guests; they will suffer
men to be drinking in their houses on the Sabbath Daye
and in time of Divine Service, which is too common a
thing. And the poor of the towne are so increased by
these houses that they know not how to live, not the
parishioners are hardly able to maintain them. Murder
hath been committed in one of these houses, and lament-
able it is to hear the fearful oaths and swearing that are
there vented. And the highways are made so deep with
brewers carting of beer there winter and summer once or
twice a week (for such good vent they have for it) that
with the ordinary six days' work they are not but half
repaired."

Both defendants were fined twenty shillings each
and sent to the House of Correction.

Drinking obviously caused disturbances in the
village, but there was also trouble with a lodging house.
In 1613 Francis Rubbard was presented to the Quarter
Sessions for offending the villagers by "keeping divers men
and women in his house as inmates, by reason whereof
there is much discord between the inmates and the

inhabitants".

Poaching was also a common crime through the centuries and it was always fair game to take wild animals from another's land. The law allowed only the owner of the land to take any animals, but much poaching was carried on that was never discovered, although a few unfortunate villagers were brought before the Courts. The Sessions of 1577 record that John Robson of Upminster with John Grace of Dagenham, gardener, broke into the Glebe land, belonging to William Washer, rector of Upminster, and caught rabbits there with 'hays', which were nets used as traps. In 1609 William Farlowe was convicted of stealing a hay worth seven pence, and a ferret worth three pence from William Latham, Gentleman: this offence would have happened on the Gaynes estate. The sentence was whipping. As well as being caught in the act it was an offence to be caught with poaching equipment: in 1674 William Marson of Upminster was presented to the Court for keeping a greyhound, a gun, nets and ferrets against the law.

An interesting case concerned William Hall of Upminster, who was the subject of a petition to the Quarter Sessions in 1602. The petition, presented by John Graygoose of Epping, recited that William Hall arranged for a child of five years of age to be lodged with John Graygoose for the period of a year or so for the sum of twenty shillings to cover board, lodging and clothing. Subsequently, Hall was executed for felony and the child was not being provided for after the period had expired. The petition goes on to ask the Court to summon the Churchwardens and Overseers of the parish of Upminster to attend the Court in order that the matter could be resolved. It is not known why Hall arranged for the child, presumbly his, to be lodged out, unless he knew he was off on his criminal exploits or, possibly, going to prison. The most probable outcome would have been that the parish of Upminster would have had to take the child back and undoubtedly he or she would have ended up as one of the parish poor.

A year later, in 1603, there is a little insight into the interior of Upminster Hall, by virtue of an eviction presented at the Quarter Sessions. The owner of Upminster Hall manor was Roger James, who had leased the estate to William Wiseman the Younger. Although the circumstances surrounding the eviction are not known, it is possible that it was for the non-payment of rent. William Wiseman the Elder and Christopher Good forcibly entered the manor house and threw out the tenant, William Wiseman the Younger, and then stayed there themselves. The court case was to obtain authority for a forcible eviction of Messrs Wiseman and Good. The entry described part of the manor house –

"... making a forcible entry into the Hall of the Manor House of Upminster, also a parlour called the Great Parlour and a room above it and a garret above the said room, another room called the Cheese Chamber and a room above it, and a garret above the said room last mentioned. A buttery, a cellar, two kitchens called the Old Kitchen and the New Kitchen and a boultinge house; another part of the house called a Milkhouse, a Brew-house, a Larder and a room above the larder and another parlour called the New Parlour..."

It can be seen that Upminster Hall was a sizeable manor house in the early 17th century.

Then, as now, straightforward theft was always in evidence, but probably with the population of the village at only 300 in 1600 detection may have been easier. Adria Jones was brought before the Sessions on 4th October, 1599, charged with –

"Adria Jones of Upminster, spinster, presented for stealing two cheeses worth two shillings, a pair of shoes worth eighteen pence, four kerchers worth four shillings, three neckerchers worth two shillings, a waistcoat worth two shillings and sixpence belonging to John Stynt at the same."

In the same year Thomas Cassell of Upminster was charged with stealing a tub worth ten pence belonging to John Burton, also of Upminster.

An interesting entry that also records the punishment was that of Mary Barrett in 1631 on 10th June stole seven hens worth ten pence, belonging to John Drywood, Gentleman: she confessed and was whipped.

Thomas Fuller, a labourer, was whipped in 1634 for stealing fourteen wheatsheaves worth five shillings from John Rigelwood.

A popular punishment of the day was transportation, which had started in the reign of Elizabeth I. An Upminster man was transported in 1830 for stealing 11 fat hogs from the Upminster Hall estate: Thomas Conn and an accomplice were tracked by a trail of blood from their cart to the forest at Havering. The accomplice went to prison and Thomas Conn left for Australia. In the same year Benjamin Fuller was convicted of stealing a smock belonging to Samuel Overall, a labourer, of Upminster. He was caught at the 'Bell' Inn at Brentwood wearing the smock: his punishment was 3 months' hard labour.

Wilson, the Upminster historian, recorded these two incidents, as he did the two robberies at St Laurence Church in 1878 and 1892. On the first occasion thieves broke in by the most westerly window in the north aisle and they stole from the church an iron chest, using a foot stool to help them. Nothing of value was stolen and, fortunately, the parish records were found nearby. The felons in the 1892 break-in forced a wooden chest, as they could not open the iron chest. Once again, the documents inside were not touched. Probably the thieves were hoping for church plate and other valuables.

An unusual occurrence concerning the church was recorded in the Quarter Sessions in 1586, when James Rowbotham, who died that April, was buried in the churchyard. Six weeks later, on 30th June, various men known to the presenters of the case to the Court dug up James Rowbotham's coffin and reburied it the following night. One wonders what all this was about, but no further clues are available.

Earlier it was noted that the Wiseman family was in trouble about an eviction and, once again, their name crops up, this time connected with their religion. The Wisemans were Catholics or Recusants and could be brought before the Archdeacon's Court for not attending the services of the Church of England. The Upminster Wisemans were related to the Wisemans of Saffron Walden and the Calendar of State Papers records that in 1594, when searches were taking place looking for people holding Catholic services, Mary Wiseman of Upminster was found in the house of Jane Wiseman of Saffron Walden, where a Mass had been prepared. The priest escaped, possibly by hiding in a priest hole, to be seen in some old country houses. Mary Wiseman was the daughter of

George Wiseman and so the sister of the William Wiseman evicted from Upminster Hall. The Wisemans, besides not attending Church of England services, were also presented to the Archdeacon's Court for allowing their servants to work during service time and for refusing to pay their tithes for the upkeep of the church.

An embarrassing situation arose in 1604 when one of the churchwardens, Richard Wigglesworth, presented his own Rector, William Washer, to the Court for letting his chancel and the Rectory fall into decay. The same year Richard Wigglesworth was presented for suspected 'incontinency' with his servant, Katherine Haldon: it rather looks as if the Rector got his own back on his Churchwarden!

While the churchwardens and the Rector would over-see the morals of the parish, the Vestry appointed a Constable every year to keep public order and to bring to court those who broke the law. However, the job was un-paid and only for a year and, being a villager himself, it is probable that occasional bribes allowed the constable to turn a blind eye to many minor misdemeanours. Originally Constables were appointed by the Lord of the Manor through his own Manor Court. In Upminster's case the Constable was appointed by the Vestry from the 16th century. The job usually fell to one of the heavyweights of the village, like the blacksmith or wheelwright. Although the appointment was made by the Vestry, it was officially ratified by a Justice in Quarter Sessions.

Whipping was a fairly common punishment and, although Upminster probably had a whipping post, there is no mention in the records, but if anywhere it would probably have been near the stocks, which were just inside the Upminster Hall boundary in Hall Lane [Station Road]. A ducking stool is mentioned in the rolls of Upminster hall manor and this would have been on the village green in front of the old 'Bell' Inn at the central crossroads. What is certain is the existence of the village cage, a small lock-up for vagrants, drunks or those awaiting an appearance before the Justices. The parish cage existed in Upminster during the 17th and 18th centuries and was again sited near the 'Bell' crossroads. The parish minutes of 1803 record that Mr Hammond was asked to prepare an estimate for building a new cage.

The total cost was to be £21.3.10d. The cage was square and about six feet wide with a pyramid-shaped roof.

The Parish Constable was responsible for presenting his accounts to the Vestry for his expenses incurred in carrying out his duties and these give an insight into some of his duties. The majority of the Constable's expenses relate to the cost of travelling to places like Brentwood, Billericay, Chelmsford or Waltum Stoo (this is the Constable's spelling of Walthamstow). These visits would have been chasing offenders, taking convicted villagers to jail or attending the Justices. Some of the accounts relate to responsibilities that should have been carried out by a churchwarden or the Overseer of the Poor, like making payments to the poor.

The Lord of the Manor of Gaynes in the 1770s was Sir James Esdaile, who had a town house at Bunhill Row, London. The Parish Constable was Richard Townsend and he charged the parish one shilling and sixpence [7½p] for visiting Sir James at his London residence, probably in connection with some crime committed on Gaynes Manor. A robbery took place at Gaynes in 1788, probably when Sir James was not in residence, because it was recorded at the Bow Street, London, police station on 16th April. The report reads – "Whereas this morning about 10 o'clock 4 men with crapes or handkerchieves over their faces and dressed in drab coloured greatcoats and armed with pistols feloniously broke open and entered the Manor House called Great Gaynes in the Parish of Upminster and stole there the following articles, viz; a silver watch, maker's name Baker, a pair of silver shoe and knee buckles, two greatcoats, one drab coloured with the buttons removed on both sides, 4 shirts and neck cloths, 2 silk handkerchieves, a £20 banknote, a large silver spoon marked R.E., as well as 7 guineas in money. Whoever will give such information to Sir Sampson Wright at the above office as may be the means of apprehending and convicting the offenders guilty of the same shall receive £50 reward from the gentleman robbed".

Sir Robert Peel did not form the Metropolitan Police, the first official force, until 1829, but Upminster still had its own unpaid constable. Prior to 1834 there were two, in that year being increased to three and, by 1842, there were eight. This large increase in policing in a village of only 1,100 people was probably due to the state of the economy at the time, which was going through a period of recession. The 1840s saw a sequence of poor harvests and rising prices, which drove more of the poor to crime, resulting in the need for more officers. Shortly thereafter residents in various areas were forming themselves into Associations, employing nighwatchmen to guard those houses where the owner was a member. The subscriptions paid for the watchman. The Constables elected by the Vestry were, of course, unpaid and consequently unwilling to undertake night duty.

Gradually the rural counties followed London's example and formed their own police forces, which Essex did in 1846, but it was not until 1886 that Upminster petitioned the Chief Constable of Essex – it received its first paid constable that year. His name was J Webb and he stayed for 10 years, on his leaving being presented with a marble clock by grateful residents. The most noteworthy policeman was Constable Beasley, who arrived in 1901 and stayed until 1917 before being transferred to Harwich. He had been promoted to Sergeant in 1912. Wilson, in his scrapbooks, makes various references to Beasley's exploits in Upminster which, although not spectacular, ensured that law and order was maintained in an expanding community. Cuttings for the years 1910 and 1911, for example, mention –
stopped a runaway horse; found dead lambs and watched until two dogs returned to worry the sheep further, beat them off and followed them home; found corpse on Upminster Hall Farm, that of Robert Shelley, a bird scarer, died of natural causes; assisted in removing a bull from Henry Talbot's greengrocer's shop in Station Road.

Until 1910 PC Beasley operated from his home, but then the Chief Constable recommended that Upminster should have its own police station. A suitable property was found in Cranham Road [now St Mary's Lane] and was purchased for £750 that September. The police station is in the same location today, although in larger premises.

MODERN DEVELOPMENT

The latter years of the 19th century saw many changes that contributed to the development of Upminster during the first 30 years of the 20th century, the like of which most of the older residents did not anticipate in their wilder dreams.

The single major development that 'opened up' Upminster was the coming of the railway. The Great Eastern line to Romford, Brentwood and beyond had been open since 1839 to Romford and as far as Colchester by 1843. The nearest station to Upminster was Harold Wood, opened in 1869, but most people used Romford as the route to London by train. The London, Tilbury & Southend line was built as far as Barking by 1854, from there it turned southwards to Tilbury and in 1882 an Act empowered the company to extend the track to Shoebury- ness. The plan was to extend from Barking to Upminster and then on to Pitsea, linking up with the Tilbury section, which had run to Southend since 1856.

The building of the Barking–Upminster section was started on 11th October, 1883, at the Upminster end, with notables travelling from Fenchurch Street to Rainham and then to Upminster by horse-drawn carriages to perform the ceremony of turning the first sod. The section was opened on 1st May, 1885, the line pushed on to East Horndon exactly one year later, and the Barking to Pitsea link was completed on 1st June, 1888. To link the Fenchurch Street and Liverpool Street lines the single track from Upminster to Grays was opened on 1st July, 1892, and the Upminster–Romford link on 7th June, 1893.

The District electric line was extended to East Ham in 1905 and to Barking in 1908, but the complete $7\frac{3}{4}$ mile route to Upminster was not opened until 12 Septem- ber, 1932.

The bus service was slow to get to Upminster and

Station Road, east side, 1910. The cottages below are on the extreme right

Cant's boot repairer and Abrahams' bakery

it was not until 1921 that the first open topped double decker buses ran from Upminster through Hornchurch and Romford to Stratford Broadway.

The opening of the railway in 1885 should have heralded Upminster's residential expansion, with trains to Fenchurch Street in half an hour or so, coupled with the delights of living on the edge of the countryside, but this was not so. The major landowners were unwilling to sell for housing development despite the profits it would bring, so for the next 15 years or so there was little change. The first major sale of land was in 1901 when Dowsing and Davis of Romford bought 10 acres on the north side of Upminster Hill, cornering Station Road. Gaynes, Branfil and Champion Roads were laid out, but by 1909 there were only 24 houses built and eventually the land was sold to W P Griggs & Co. in 1911. This firm of builders had begun developing years earlier in the Ilford and Walthamstow areas and, when W G Key joined the firm in 1897 he built the Cranbrook and Clementswood estates in Ilford. The firm moved into Upminster with Key as its guiding light at about the time Dowsing and Davis started building. The shops in Station Road were built in 1907 and, soon after, the Hall Lane estate commenced with Deyncourt, Engayne, Courtenay and Waldegrave Gardens all developing slowly. Peter Griggs of this firm of builders, later to become Sir Peter, planned to develop 700 acres of the Upminster Hall estate as a Garden Suburb. On the north side of the railway the houses were all to be built in a half an acre of land each, while on the south side there were to be shops and smaller houses. Prices in 1906/7 ranged from £450 to £1,150. During 1906 44 houses were built or were in course of construction and by 1909 the total was 96. All were private residences, except for a preparatory school and a doctor's house. On the south side the shops opposite Roome's Stores were quickly followed in 1907 by St Lawrence and Howard Roads, where 79 houses had been built by 1909.

The Hall Lane estate extended as far as Ingrebourne Gardens, after which the land was still held by the owners of Upminster Hall. The name Ingrebourne Gardens was not well received by the Parish Council and at a meeting in 1912 it was proposed that W P Griggs and Co. be asked whether they would be prepared to alter the name in view of the other references to Ingrebourne in the village. This name was not changed, but a principal road in the village did alter its name ten years later when the road from the parish boundary at the bottom of Upminster Hill was renamed St Mary's Lane: previously the section from the river to the centre of the village had been called Upminster Hill and the section onwards to the Cranham boundary was Cranham Lane.

The main agent selling the new properties in the 1910s and 1920s was Upminster Estates, Ltd., who had offices in Station Road near the railway bridge on the western side. Upminster was referred to by the salesmen as Upminster Garden Suburb and Upminster Estates, in their 26 page brochure of the 1920s advertising the new properties, describes Upminster thus –

"The village of Upminster, happily placed away from the principal roads leading out of London, has, for that reason, managed to preserve its homely and old-world characteristics, although barely fifteen miles from the city. Situated south of the railway, and within some two minutes walk of the station, the old village, with its quaint church, is well worthy of a visit. Retracing one's steps and crossing the railway bridge, one takes the beautiful winding road called Upminster Hall Lane, which leads northwards from the station for nearly two miles through the centre of this richly wooded Estate, and thence to the Common, Great Warley and Brentwood. No wayfarer can fail to be charmed by the quiet, rural beauty of this park-like Estate, with its extensive views over a large expanse of undulating country, or to at once agree that there is no more delightful place in our Home Counties, or one more worthy to be described as the beauty spot of Essex."

All the development during the period 1900-24 was in the Station Road/Hall Lane area and its environs. Corbets Tey Road in the 1920s was still a country lane with cottages and houses on the side where the shops are now. St Mary's Lane was still a country lane with a few cottages and shops that petered out after a couple of hundred yards on coming to the New Place estate.

At the same time as Griggs was developing the Hall Lane and station areas he had also bought, in 1909, New Place and its 70 acres of land, but it was not until the last occupant's death in 1924 that development started. The house itself was demolished, but the stables (the Clock House) and the gardens and moat behind were retained as parish offices and a small public park. The boundaries of the estate became Sunnyside Gardens and Argyle Gardens, with the Junior and Infants' School forming the other boundary in St Mary's Lane.

On the death of Henry Joslin in 1927 his whole estate of 400 acres, comprising much of the land on either side of Corbets Tey Road was put up for sale as one lot. It failed to sell in this way, and so, in 1929, it was broken up into 17 lots, the most significant of which were Gaynes House and estate grounds of 105 acres (Gaynes Park Road and Little Gaynes Lane); Hoppy Hall farm of 92 acres (Southview Drive and the 'tree' roads); Hunt's farm (Springfield Gardens) of 130 acres; and Tadlows farm (Cranston Park Avenue) of 66 acres. The balance of the total acreage was houses and cottages facing Corbets Tey Road and in Little Gaynes Lane.

During the 1930s extensive building development took place on both sides of Corbets Tey Road and, by the time that building stopped with the outbreak of war in 1939, central Upminster was fully developed. It is worth repeating the population figures that reflect the growth in house building in the 20th century – 1901, 1,477; 1911, 2,468; 1921, 3,559; 1931, 5,732; 1941, no census; 1951, 13,038.

After the war building was principally in the north of the parish in the Avon Road area and during the 1950s and 1960s the majority of the houses in the River Drive estate were constructed.

The first shopping development of any consequence were the shops on the east of Station Road, which still bear the building date of 1907 on their facade. This side of the road was fully developed by 1909, with shops all the way down to the cross-roads, although those between St Lawrence Road and the 'Bell' were older than the others. From St Lawrence Road southwards came Battson, the dairy (later United Dairies), then Dales, the news-agent (later Ramseys, now Martins), then Caldicotts and Talbots, plumbers and wheelwrights respectively, and this was followed by the National School, where the National Westminster Bank is now. Before the next block of shops was built housing Lloyds Bank on the corner, there was Mr Jupp's butchers shop and, sticking out into the cross-roads, was the Cosy Corner Cafe.

On the other side of the road, starting from the Station, were a couple of houses which comprised Grigg's Upminster Estates office and this was followed by the Crumpled Horn Dairy (now the Post Office) and then came Doctor Bedsoe's large house on the corner of Branfil Road. From Branfil Road to Gaynes Road there was nothing in the early days until the British School (girls), which was where Barclay's Bank is situated. After the school came Cant's, the shoe repairer, located on the side of a small row of cottages, at the other end of which was Abraham's the bakers. Then came Aggiss' Garage and, finally, Mr Aggiss' house and garden on the corner of the crossroads.

St Mary's Lane had no shops at all in the early 1900s, as the land on one side was owned by the Upmin-ster Hall estate and on the other by New Place manor. The shops on both sides and the school were built in the 1920/30s.

The only shop in Corbets Tey Road was the Post Office among Post Office Cottages, which eventually changed to Wilson's Store, and was sited where Wool-worth's is today. The shops on both sides of Corbets Tey Road were built in the 1930s when the Springfield and Gaynes estates were developed, although the block of shops between Woolworths and West Lodge were not completed until after World War II.

Upminster is not rich in public houses. The 'Bell' Inn stood at the central crossroads opposite the church for centuries until it was pulled down in 1961. This was the oldest public house in Upminster being originally built prior to 1636. Older residents will recall the 'Bell' right on the corner by the traffic lights, but the previous building was further back on the side of the village green that existed in the Middle Ages. The other central Upminster public house was the 'Mason's Arms', which was rebuilt in 1928. The 'White Hart' in Hacton Lane first opened in 1854, when two cottages were converted: at the time Hacton had a little community of its own and justified a public house. Although there are fewer houses in Hacton now, thanks to the motor car the

APRIL 1909

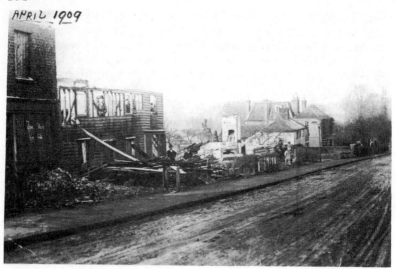

Upminster Hill. Cottages, including 'The Compasses' being demolished, 1909.
Red House in the background

Crumpled Horn Dairy and Tea Garden

The Crumpled Horn Dairy (now the Post Office) about 1926

'White Hart' still thrives today, despite competition from the 'Optimist', only a quarter of a mile away, that was built in 1956. The 'Huntsman and Hounds' at Corbets Tey was originally a 17th century pub, which was rebuilt in 1896. The only other public house in Upminster at the turn of this century was the 'Shepherd and Dog' in Shepherd's Hill, Harold Wood: although this hostelry is not now within the postal district of Upminster, it was within Upminster's parish boundary in the early part of the 20th century.

Other establishments that once existed in Upminster and Corbets Tey, but have long since closed, are 'The Compasses', a beerhouse on the south side of Upminster Hill near Boundary Road, opened 1845, closed 1870; "George Inn", Corbets Tey, opposite the 'Huntsman and Hounds', first known licensee 1769, closed 1901; "Anchor", Harwood Hall Lane, next to High House, the original building still stands as a private house, opened 17th century, closed 1896; "The Cock", Hacton Lane, open in 1743, but probably earlier, closed about 1785.

The Parish Council had purchased the Clock House in St Mary's Lane as council offices in 1924 and meetings were held there for the following ten years, until the Parish Council was swallowed by the Hornchurch Urban District in 1934. A couple of years later the Clock House was converted into a County Branch Library and ambulance garage and remained as such until 1963 when the new library was opened in Corbets Tey Road. It is now an old people's residence.

The village Post Office changed its position a number of times and there are recorded four separate locations. The first, as mentioned earlier in this chapter, was in Corbets Tey Road, then it was in St Mary's Lane on the Yorkshire Wool Shop corner opposite the church, where recently a new development of offices and shops has been built. From there the Post Office moved from 1910 to 1938 to Station Road, into the rear of Green's Stores on the north corner of Howard Road: Then it moved across the road to its present premises in what was originally the Crumpled Horn Dairy.

Above Green's Stores Upminster's first telephone exchange opened in 1922, but due to the fast development of the village in the 1920s, a new exchange was built in

1929 in St Mary's Lane, which has now been superceded by another exchange further down the road past Argyle Gardens.

The Local Government Act of 1894 saw the setting up of Upminster Parish Council and one of the powers conferred on Parish Councils was authority to provide men and equipment to fight fires and form a Fire Brigade. Long before the Act Hornchurch Vestry had provided fire-fighting equipment, which must have been very basic, in 1830. By the early 20th century Hornchurch was very well organised with fire hydrants strategically placed, a new fire engine and, eventually, its own fire station in Billet Lane in 1907. Upminster had nothing at all and, when in 1903, Hornchurch wrote suggesting a share of equipment, the Clerk at Upminster wrote back saying that, as there were no hydrants in Upminster, there was no point in any co-operation. Consequently, any fires in Upminster had to be dealt with by Hornchurch in the best way they could. However, by 1908 seven fire hydrants were installed and a fire brigade started.

The first 'engine' was a cart, probably pushed, with Upminster Parish Council painted on the side. The hose had brass fittings and was stamped 'U.P.C.' It is clear from correspondence that all was not harmony between the parish councils of Upminster and Hornchurch on the subject of fire brigades: apparently the two parishes could not agree on the question of co-operation and so Hornchurch wrote to Upminster saying that now the latter had its own equipment they would not attend any fires in the Upminster area. Upminster's reply was that they hoped that there would be co-operation notwithstanding that agreement could not be reached.

The incident that brought matters to a head was the fire at Martyn's Farm on the Branfil estate in Hall Lane in September, 1911. As there were no hydrants in the area the Upminster brigade could do nothing and it was left to Hornchurch with their more modern equipment to deal with the fire, but not before much damage had been done.

It was clear to Upminster's council that they needed the support of Hornchurch's better equipment and so an agreement was finally reached that Upminster Parish Council would pay Hornchurch Parish Council

£5.5.0d for the fire engine and £2.2.0d for the horses every time Hornchurch attended a fire in Upminster. A fee of ten shillings was also to be paid for the use of the hose. The corollary applied if Upminster's brigade attended a fire in Hornchurch.

There should have been no further problems, but in 1912 there was a fire at Upminster Common. When the Hornchurch brigade arrived they realised the fire was in the parish of Upminster and so a bill for £11.16.8d was remitted. Upminster refused to pay and a new dispute arose as to who should decide when the Hornchurch brigade should attend an Upminster fire. Upminster felt that Hornchurch should only be called out when they received a call from the officer in charge at Upminster. Hornchurch did not agree, but bowed to Upminster's insistence. The problems between the two fire brigades seem to have been solved, as no further incidents were reported. In 1925 a retired professional fireman, John Bridger, was appointed as Captain, improving the efficiency of the volunteer force and two years later the parish bought the brigade a motorised fire engine in place of the hand truck. The brigade was based at the council offices at the Clock House.

Although there were not enough fire hydrants for the fire brigade a mains water supply had been made available by the South Essex Waterworks Company from 1863, when the main passed through Upminster en route from Grays to Romford. Initially, the water main supplemented the various sources of spring water, although it was not until 1909 that the Upminster Common area received a supply of mains water.

With the increase in housing development sewerage disposal became a problem. The first sewerage scheme was in 1899 at Upminster Bridge, but after several extensions a new works was built in 1922 at Bury Farm, Great Warley, to serve Upminster and Cranham.

Another difficulty connected with the growth of Upminster was dust. The Parish Council minutes of April, 1924, record a request that Romford Rural District Council, of which Upminster wa a member, be asked to water the roads on Sundays because of the dust arising from the increase in motor traffic in Upminster. The council considered that the dust blown around by the cars was a health hazard.

In 1931 the council wrote to the Essex County Council about, amongst other noises, the new problem of 'audible wireless installations', when the radio had progressed from head phones: the council was enquiring whether there was a bye-law which could stop this nuisance.

The Romford Gas and Coke Company laid gas mains to Upminster in 1872, although gas street lighting did not arrive until 1905. Electrity did not come until 1926, which means that much of the early housing development was lit by gas.

Education in Upminster in the 19th century was thriving and in Chapter 3 the development of the British School and the National School, both opened in 1851, was traced. In 1928 the existing Junior and Infants' School was built, but the steady increase in Upminster's population forced the school to be enlarged in 1932 and, by 1934, the National School was opened again to take the overflow. Up to 1936 all children up to school leaving age were educated at St Mary's Lane, but that year Gaynes County Secondary School was built in Brackendale Gardens and from then only children up to the age of 11 were taught at the 'Bell' School. Gaynes School opened with 480 senior pupils, the catchment area including Cranham and North and South Ockendon. The school has been enlarged on many occasions over subsequent years as the population grew.

In Cedar Avenue, Branfil School was built in 1943 and intially it was a temporary school for 100 infants, part of the building being used as the new Hornchurch County High School. When the grammar school moved away to new premises off Wingletye Lane in 1954 the whole of the premises became a junior and infants' school.

The Sacred Heart of Mary secondary school for girls at Hill Place, Upminster Hill, opened as a boarding school in 1927, but in the 1950s reverted to being a day school. St Joseph's Roman Catholic Primary School in St Mary's Lane opened just after the 1939/45 war in a house called Mavisbank and on the same site in 1956 new classrooms were built. The Coopers' Company and Coburn mixed secondary school moved from Bow during the period

1971-74 to new buildings in St Mary's Lane towards Cranham, owing to the difficulty in recruiting children in the Bow area.

The development of modern Upminster cannot be considered without mentioning the growth of the church.

St Laurence Church suffered from two problems, the first the growth of the population, making it clear that the present church was inadequate and, also for the same reason, the lack of space in the churchyard. By 1902 the churchyard was full, though not until 1926 did the rector give a piece of his garden north of the nave, abutting St Mary's Lane for use as a burial ground. From 1928 to 1935 extensive alterations and additions were made to the east end of the church, with the removal of the chancel and the building of a new choir aisle and sanctuary, together with St George's Chapel on the south side and the Lady Chapel at the east end of the north aisle. The last additions were the sacristy and the choir vestry.

Roman Catholicism can be traced back to the Reformation, but it was not until Countess Helen Tasker bought Minster House in 1880/1 that services were again held regularly in the parish. Minster House was adjacent to Hill Place on Upminster Hill and in this property Canon J Kyne of Brentwood opened a small oratory and conducted services. Although the Canon died in 1881 services continued until 1888, when the property was sold after the Countess' death. There was a gap then until 1923 when, through the efforts of the Revd. Julius Van Meenen, the church of St Joseph first opened its doors. The original building was in St Mary's Lane, on the corner of Sunnyside Gardens until 1932, when a site was acquired in Champion Road. For a start there was a temporary church there until the present edifice was built in 1939.

The Congregational Church (United Reform) is by far the oldest non-conformist church in Upminster, with a history dating back to at least 1799. Various people in Upminster during the 19th century registered their houses for independent worship before the Chapel was opened on Upminster Hill. The Chapel, next to Hill Place, was sold to the Plymouth Bretheren in 1910 when a much larger church in the Gothic style was built in Station Road on the corner of Gaynes Road in 1911.

The Methodist (Wesleyan) Church originated in 1910 in a temporary corrugated iron building, although it was as early as 1848 that Robert Eaglen, a Brentwood preacher, registered a house for Methodist worship. The first members of the present Methodist Church met for worship in a drawing room above the pharmacy in Station Road: older residents may remember Mr & Mrs Humphreys, who ran the chemists shop. The corrugated building in Hall Lane, on the site of the present church, was given by Methodists of Goodmayes on land bought for £600. The building was popularly known as the 'tin tabernacle'. In 1923 a new church was built in Tudor Gothic style, with enlargements in 1935.

The last of the principal churches to open in Upminster was the Baptist Church in Springfield Gardens. Support came from the North Street, Hornchurch, Baptist Church and in 1935 a school and chapel was built with 33 members. Membership rose to 133 in 1945 and to 257 by 1973. The new church was built in 1959.

The Congregational Church, 1911

CRANHAM

A history of Upminster would not be complete without reference to Cranham for the two parishes are closely linked geographically, even if not so historically until recently with housing development running continuously from one to the other.

Cranham is a much smaller parish than Upminster, although the shape is very similar. Whereas Upminster parish was 6 miles long from the Upminster Common area down to the Aveley border, Cranham only extends for 3 miles from a line about one mile north of the A127 to where the Ockendon Road joins Clay Tye Road. The eastern boundary is roughly on the line of the M25 motorway. The western boundary is, of course, Upminster's eastern boundary, though it does not extend as far south. The old parish of Cranham had an acreage of 1,879, compared to Upminster's 3,375.

The Domesday Book of 1086 contains the first record of Cranham. There were two manors in the parish, one called Ockendon (Wochenduna) and the other Cranham (Craohu). The Domesday Book entries read –

Wochenduna (Cranham or Ockendon Episcopi) was held by Alvric in King Edward's time as a manor of 3 hides and 40 acres. Now Hugh holds it of the Bishop [of London]. Then 6 villeins; now 8. Then 5 bordars; now 15. Then 6 serfs; now 4. Then, as now, 3 ploughs on the demesne and 4 ploughs belonging to the men. Woodland for 500 swine and 20 acres of meadow. There are 4 colts, 144 sheep and 20 beasts. Then and afterwards it was worth four pounds, now six.

Craohu (Cranham) was held by Alwin, a free man, as a manor and as 1½ hides, is held now of the Bishop [Odo of Bayeux] by Hugh. Then, as now, 1 villein and 1 bordar. Then 1 plough; now half a one. Woodland for 100 swine and 1½ acres of meadow. Then and afterwards it was worth 50 shillings; now 20.

A similar exercise as that in Chapter 1 can be carried out to find the size of Cranham's two manors. The hide, it will be recalled, is roughly 120 acres, while 26 pigs occupied an average 100 acres. Relating this to Cranham's Domesday statistics the figures work out that Wochenduna was of 400 acres, plus meadow of 20 acres, and woodland for swine of 1,923 acres, totalling about 2,350 acres; Craohu had 180 acres, plus 1½ acres of meadow and 385 acres of woodland, totalling about 565 acres.

The records indicate that the ancient parish of Cranham had 1,879 acres, but these calculations exceed this number of over 1,000 acres. The similar sum for Upminster came out about right. The suspect figure has to be the Wochenduna woodland acreage which is only an estimate based on the number of pigs on the land. It is possible that on this particular manor the swine did not enjoy such a large area and if, for example, the manor put 50 pigs to the acre, this would reduce Wochenduna's size by about 900 acres and would be much nearer the known extent.

The other surprising piece of information, to support the Domesday entries, was the number of men working on the two manors. In total in 1086 there were 29, compared with 34 for Upminster. Considering that Upminster's acreage is twice that of Cranham, it is un-expected that Cranham had such a large population. Maybe, therefore, Cranham in the 11th century was a lot larger and the 2,900 acres calculated above was correct, which then follows that it could support the men (and their families) listed in Domesday. The total population, based on 29 working men, with wives and children, comes out at about 150, which seems rather high considering the population in 1801 was only 240. It does rather look that Cranham's boundaries were more extensive nine hundred years ago.

The location of the manors has proved difficult in Cranham's case. No one has any idea where the smaller manor was, although the *Victoria History of Essex* bel-ieves that the larger manor was sited in the north of the parish, although Cranham Hall, which eventually became the manor house, is in the southern half. The manor of

Wochenduna was one of 18 held by the Bishop of London after the Conquest. The Bishop probably never even set foot in the parish, although the See continued to receive rent from Cranham until the end of the 16th century.

The smaller manor of Craohu was in the possession of Bishop Odo of Bayeux, who, incidentally, held the small manor in Upminster in the south of the parish. Odo had 40 manors in Essex alone until 1088, when he was exiled and forfeited all his land. It seems that the Bishop of London 'acquired' various manors previously owned by Bishop Odo, particularly those adjacent to his own land. This appears to be the case in Cranham as, after 1088, the Bishop of London is the only recorded tenant in chief covering the whole of Cranham. Once again, as with the other manor in Cranham, the under tenant was Hugh. There is little recorded for this small manor in later centuries: up to the late 13th century there are various references to tenants and to rent paid. In 1272 the yearly rent was eight shillings [40p]. Nothing is recorded later than this and probably the manor was incorporated into its larger neighbour of Ockendon. As can be seen from the names of the two manors, they were at some time both called Cranham. Although the larger manor was called Cranham in the time of Edward IV (1461-83) it was originally called Ockendon (Wochenduna) and then Bishop's Ockendon to distinguish it from the adjacent manors of North and South Ockendon.

The Ockendon family held the larger manor from the 12th to 14th centuries, but were still under-tenants of the Bishop of London. After the Ockendons came Sir Nicholas de Halughton and then his heirs, who gave way to Sir Ralph St Leger. Cranham appears to have got its name in the 15th century from a report that there were cranes in the area. The hawking of cranes was a popular pastime then. The second part of the village name possibly derives from 'hoh' or ridge, referring to the raised ground running east to west across the parish where Cranham Hall and the church are sited. Alternatively, Cranham may have got its name from being called 'the place of crows'.

The succession of Ockendon manor from when records began looks something like this -

     1066   Alvric

1086	Bishop of London
12th-14th	Ockendon family
1337	Sir Nicholas de Halughton
1363	Sir Ralph St Leger
1425	Sir John Lewis and family

1471   Richard, Duke of Gloucester (brother of Edward IV and later Richard III)

1487   Lewis family again (leased to the Lathams of Upminster)

1571   Sir William Petre of Ingatestone and family (780 acres)

1647   Nathan Wright and family. Bought for £6,100, but $\frac{2}{3}$ of the proceeds confiscated from the Petre family for not attending Church of England services (recusants)

1743   General James Oglethorpe (owned by Mrs Oglethorpe)

1787   Sir Thomas H Apreece, Bt., and family

1852   Samuel Gurney of Overend, Norfolk (of Gurney & Co., bankers). Bought for £31,000.

1867   George Rastwick - bought manor house only and not the whole estate of 940 acres (half of Cranham!)

Richard Benyon purchased 812 acres of the manor farm land.

1937   Southend on Sea Estate Company bought Cranham Hall and Cranham Lodge, with 415 acres, for £54,000.

Although it is known that the Bishop of London was tenant in chief (under the King) until the 16th century and those listed above until that time were under tenants, it is probable that from Sir William Petre onwards the names are the owners, not tenants, although it is not known when the Crown ceased to have an interest in the manor. By comparison it is noted that in 1419 'the king's hand was removed from Gaynes', although the King's brother had an interest in Cranham in 1471. It was probably in the time of the Lewis or Petre families that they became freeholders, as we know the term today, and no longer had any obligation to the Crown.

Although it was said earlier that the smaller manor in Cranham at the time of the Domesday survey was probably incoporated into the larger manor, a new manor evolved growing to 460 acres, although part of this estate was in the parish of Great Warley. The manor lay in the north of the parish in Beredens Lane, which runs to

Warley. In 1357 the Ockendon family conveyed to John de Berden land in the parish of Cranham and this small estate was increased by the purchase of a further 52 acres when Sir Ralph de St Leger held Ockendon manor. By 1453 the estate was 334 acres, but by 1523 it had fallen to 213, although increasing again later. The Roche family bought the manor in 1523 and, when a daughter of the family married Ralph Latham, this family took over this manor, along with its neighbouring manor at Upminster Hall. Latham sold Beredens in 1641 and the manor passed through various hands until 1801, when it was sold for £8,230 with 460 acres. During the next century the size of the estate fell due to a family partition and by 1918 the acreage was down to 248, when it was sold and became part of the Goldings estate in Great Warley. The manor house, off Beredens Lane was occupied by a member of the Petre family in the 1920s and was destroyed by a bomb in World War II.

Cranham boasted few major houses. In the Middle Ages there were the two manor houses, one of which disappeared in the 13th century to be replaced by Beredens in the 14th. Cranham Hall, near the church, still stands today. Cranham's population was very small in the 14th-17th centuries, with only about 50 to 150 people living in the parish. Apart from the two manor houses there were only a few small farms and cottages, none of which owned or rented many acres. The Chapman & Andre map of Essex of 1777 names only three properties and, once again, these are the manor houses of Cranham Hall and Beredens and also Cranham Parsonage. By this time the original larger manor of Wochenduna had, for some reason, moved from the north of the parish to a new site at Cranham Hall.

Cranham Parsonage was sited where Rectory Gardens is now and, as the name suggests, was the residence of the Rector. Front Lane and Moor Lane were, in 1777, called Cranham Lane and Cranham Back Lane respectively and they met again in the north of the parish where Beredens and Folkes Lanes meet today. The reason the northern parts of these lanes have changed their names is due to their being bisected by the A127. Beredens manor house was sited a little further up Beredens Lane after the convergence of the two lanes.

The Ordnance Survey map covering Upminster and Cranham published in 1872 shows no change at all from 1777, as far as the larger properties are concerned, although the population increased from about 200 to 437 in 1871. The change appears to be merely extra cottages and smallholdings springing up in Front Lane and Moor Lane, which these roads were now called.

Cranham Hall was certainly in existence in its present location by 1600, when it was a brick-built house. A new manor house was built in 1800, incorporating a small part of the original building. Additions were made both in the 19th century and again in 1904.

The best-known person to reside in Cranham was General James Oglethorpe, who married in 1743 Elizabeth Wright, heiress of Cranham Hall. James Oglethorpe was born in 1696 and was initially a soldier serving in the Austrian-Turkish War under Prince Eugene, before going into politics and becoming M.P. for Hazelmere. He was a good campaigner for the oppressed, whether they be protestant minorities in Europe or prisoners in the notorious debtor prisons. Through this interest he was appointed Chairman of a committee to inspect and report on prisons, out of which came a scheme to found a new colony called Georgia, to which would be sent prisoners and their families to start a new life.

A Royal Charter was granted by George II in 1732 and Oglethorpe sailed with 35 families from Gravesend to explore himself the Savannah River and to choose the site for the first settlement. His mission was successful and, besides founding the colony, he made friends with the Indians and brought one of their chiefs back to England to present him at Court. Oglethorpe's second expedition was a much larger affair and accompanying the flotilla of ships were John and Charles Wesley, who spent some time preaching to the settlers. In the new colony of Georgia Oglethorpe forbad slavery, drinking and the exploitation of the Indians. The General is best known for his colonisation of Georgia, but is more honoured for the defence of the new colony when hostilities broke out between Britain and Spain in 1739. Georgia being the southernmost state, it was immediately threatened by Spanish America and so Oglethorpe was appointed General Officer Commanding the British Forces. He won a convincing victory by

James Oglethorpe   by permission of the National Portrait Gallery, London

repulsing the invaders at the Battle of the Bloody Marsh.

He returned to England again in 1743 and married Elizabeth Wright, taking up residence at Cranham Hall. Two years later, while raising troops for Georgia, he was called upon to march against the rebels led by Charles Edward Stuart. His detachment did not see action and the General was subsequently courtmartialled for failing to do his duty. He was acquitted, but obviously disillusioned and consequently did not return to Georgia, although remaining Governor until 1752. He was also a Member of Parliament until 1754. He retired from public life at the age of 58, spending his remaining days farming his wife's estate at Cranham Hall and entertaining personalities like Oliver Goldsmith and Dr Samuel Johnson. He died in 1785 at the age of 89 and is buried in the family vault in the centre of the Chancel of All Saints Church, Cranham.

Cranham was principally a farming community and, in 1839, Cranham Hall and Beredens farmed 474 and 337 acres respectively. These two manors alone made up about half of the parish, the balance being farms and small-holdings none of which was larger than 100 acres. In the 15th century there are various references to a windmill, which would appear to have been sited in the north of the parish on the rising ground on the Beredens estate: no reference is found after 1464.

Like Upminster, the parish is rich in brick earth and in 1839 there is reference to a Brick Field Hollow on the Beredens land. However, by far the largest employer of labour, even including those employed on the two large manor estates, was the company that operated the Cranham brick works. They were not built until 1900 though and one wonders where the 70 employed worked before. They probably scraped a living off their own land until Colliers, Ltd., came along and developed the brick fields. Cranham's population at the time was still only about 400, so those working at the brickworks comprised a very large proportion of the working population. W H Collier also owned brick works at Shenfield, Hutton and Marks Tey. The works were fairly short-lived and closed in 1920. It is said that the clay diggings became flooded due to spring water seepage, the works being at low level. For many years these water-filled pits were a favourite haunt of schoolboys in the 1930s and 40s, before finally being filled in. There were one or two drownings in these tempting pits due to submerged machinery and the weeds.

The brick works were sited where Cranham Playing Fields are today and a map of about 1915 shows extensive works, kilns and pits covering an area of $11\frac{1}{2}$ acres with railway sidings leading into the Upminster-Southend line. The kilns were alongside the sidings to make transportation easier. Besides the track for vehicles into Moor Lane, a footpath led due south across the railway line, as it still does today, and alongside the fields joining St Mary's Lane opposite the 'Thatched House' public house. The path would obviously save the villagers working at the brickworks a long walk up to Wantz Bridge and into Moor Lane via Front Lane, if they lived in the south of the village.

The poor of the parish were always a problem, as has been seen in Upminster, and due credit must be given to those running parish affairs for doing all they could to relieve the suffering. The Vestry was responsible for the poor, but as early as 1657 it is recorded that Nathan Wright had given almshouses for two persons in St Mary's Lane: these had disappeared by the 19th century. A 'parish house' or poor house was first mentioned in 1782, when the Vestry paid 8 shillings for providing a loom for the poor. Although Cranham had its own poor house, it was obviously very small and could not accommodate all the poor of the parish. There are various references to Cranham's poor being sent to other villages, presumably for a charge, and between 1786 and 1788 three of Cranham's poor were being looked after in Great Warley's workhouse. Between 1797 and 1816 up to ten of Cranham's poor were in Upminster's workhouse, but this arrangement was not renewed after the latter date, as there were no longer any places available. Cranham's workhouse had its own resident master and wife who, it is recorded in the history of Cranham church, came to Cranham from South Ockendon to take up the post. The church has the record book kept by the master, which records the daily menus, expenses and general comments relating to the workhouse.

In 1825 Cranham was once again sending its poor to other villages, but it is uncertain whether this was the overflow or because the workhouse had closed. Whatever the situation previously, in 1828 the vestry petitioned Sir Thomas Apreece, the then Lord of the Manor, for a grant of land on which to build a new workhouse. The price of the land was £20 and the site was where the 'Jobber's Rest' public house is today, the piece of land being 36 feet deep, with a frontage to St Mary's Lane of 174 feet. The actual building was 51 feet long by 20 feet wide, with a spring water well outside. The number of inmates during the workhouse's short life of eight years was between 12 and 18, including a high proportion of children. In 1833, for example, the inmates were 3 men, 7 women and 8 children. The passing of the Poor Law Amendment Act, 1834, saw the beginning of the end of local workhouses and, like Upminster, Cranham's poor were transferred to Oldchurch, Romford, in 1836, to come under the supervision of the Romford Union. The purchaser of the workhouse, who had also bought Upminster's, was George Rowe, for the sum of £205, the proceeds going to the Romford Union and not the parish Vestry who had supplied the money only a few years before.

The first reference to a church in Cranham occurs in 1254 and the first rector listed is John de Wokydon in 1310. From these early days, up to the 18th century, the right to appoint the Rector passed with the lordship of Cranham Hall. Later the advowson was sold by one rector to another, for with it went the right to collect tithes from the villagers. In 1254 the value was 15 marks, in 1535 it was about £14, but by the 18th century the value of tithes was £130, a large sum in those days. In 1839, following the Tithe Commutation Act of 1836, Cranham's tithes were converted into cash after a survey of the village. The value to the rector then was £560, compared with Upminster's £1,052 p.a. These amounts related directly to the village acreages of 1,878 in Cranham and 3,369 in Upminster.

As Cranham was a small parish the Rector was often the incumbent at another parish. When Thomas Crosby was presented to the living in 1590 he was also Rector of Thaxted, where he resided and died. Cranham was ministered by curates, whose names appeared in the registers on behalf of the rector. The unrest in the church at the time of Protector Cromwell (1649-60) is reflected by the blanks in the church records both in the years preceeding the Commonwealth and also during the Protectorate. Even after the Reformation all was not well in Cranham. A Puritan minister, John Yardley, was thrown out in 1662, because of his non-conformity. Unfortunately, from the time of Charles II to the early 19th century absent Rectors were the order of the day, with the exception of John Woodrooffe (1735-86). Thomas Ludbey held the living from 1818-59 and, as Cranham did not have a resident landowner at Cranham Hall at this time, Ludbey became the leader of the parish community.

The church that was built in the 13th century lasted until 1873, when the present church was built and dedicated again to All Saints. At the time of the re-building the living was in the hands of St John's College, Oxford, and Cranham became one of the churches to which former fellows of that College were appointed rector. A survey was conducted by the College in the early 1870s and in view of the very dilapidated nature of the church it was decided to rebuild. The cost of the new church was £5,114, most of which was donated by Richard Benyon of Cranham Hall. Various monuments from the old church were replaced, including the marble tablet to General Oglethorpe and various brass inscriptions. The bells are dated 1460 and the three were rehung in the new church.

The district of Cranham Park was formed in 1957 with the building of St Lukes, services being held for two years previously in a builder's hut.

Protestant non-conformity came to Cranham in 1672 in the shape of John Yardley, ejected from the Church of England for his views ten years earlier. Yardley was granted a licence to preach when living at South Weald and most probably preached in Cranham, where two houses had been licenced for Presbyterian worship. A Congregational minister from Chelmsford preached in a licensed house in 1835. In the 1950s the Bretheren registered Moor Lane Chapel for worship and the Baptists built their church in Severn Drive in 1957. The builder's hut that served the Cranham Park residents so well prior to St Lukes being built was also used by the Bretheren and the Baptists before their permanent churches were ready.

The administration of the parish of Cranham, like Upminster and all other parishes, was undertaken in the Middle Ages by the Lord of the Manor through the Manor Court. Records of the manorial court exist from 1577 almost uninterrupted to the 20th century and these documents can be found in the Essex Record Office. Later the administration was undertaken by the Vestry, comprising the main figures of the community, including the Rector: once again, the original Vestry Minutes, and Overseers and Surveys Reports, together with Rate books covering various periods from 1643 onwards are all to be found in the Record Office.

The village boasted two constables between 1646 and 1660 and usually one or two thereafter: there were also two surveyors of the highways. Reading the Minutes of the Vestry or one of its sub-committees as long ago as two hundred years it is pleasing to note that, even in those uneducated and difficult times, there were suffic- ient sensible people in the parish to run the community and, at the same time, to administer to the poor of the parish.

The Local Government Act, 1894, required an elected Parish Council to be set up, which duly came about and, like Upminster, this existed until 1933, when both parishes were brought into the Hornchurch Urban District.

Before 1818 there was no formal education in Cranham, but then the Boyd Church of England School was founded by the Boyd family of Cranham Hall, in con- junction with Thomas Ludbey, the Rector, who had also taken up the living that year. There being no village school house classes were held in the cottage belonging to the first schoolmistress, Mrs Sarah Hunwicks, who taught from 1818 to 1874. The Rector established a Sunday School in 1819. For the day school the charge was four pence a week, but if the child's parents could not afford the fee, then half the cost would be paid by the church or gentlemen of the parish. The Rector reported on one occasion that the girls were regular attenders at the day school, but the boys were often absent, especially at seed time when they were wanted to keep the birds off the fields. Thomas Ludbey also recorded that, besides contributions towards the school fees, the church often made donations towards the clothing of children in need. By 1839 sixteen children were being taught in the day school, which was a very small proportion of the children of school age, considering that the population of the village was then 300. In 1847 the numbers had increased to 29 (9 boys and 20 girls).

After the teacher's cottage was pulled down in 1854 the children were taught in a wooden building also used for the Sunday School and for Evening Classes (It is surprising to find Evening Classes a hundred years ago, as we think of them as being a modern innovation). Finally, in 1870, the first purpose-built school was erected in the village, together with a teacher's house, which still stand today in St Mary's Lane between Front Lane and Chester Avenue.

The School was built as a memorial to Sarah Boyd, who had done so much for education in the village. Richard Benyon of Cranham Hall donated the site and paid part of the building costs. Until she moved away from Cranham in 1889 Miss Boyd remained in control; she died, aged 96, in 1897.

When first built the school could take 115 children, but during the 20th century the school grew in size as the population increased. An Education Report of 1916 described it as a bad school, needing regular supervision. Presumably this referred more to the quality of the teaching than the ability of the children, although the latter must have suffered from the shortcomings of the former. In 1938 the school was taken over by Essex County Council and finally closed in 1950 when Oglethorpe Primary School opened. Engayne Primary School opened in 1958 and Hall Mead Secondary School in 1960.

The population of the village grew only slowly over the centuries, which is not surprising for, as a farming community, there was nothing to draw people to the village, as the land could support only so many farms or smallholdings. It was not until the brickworks were opened in 1900 that the population started to increase, followed by housing development on the break-up of the Benyon estate. From available records Cranham's population has been -

1086   29 men (say 150 people)

1327	13 names on Tax List (probably land owners, although many others did not pay taxes)
1523	16 names on Tax List
1679	24 houses (say 150 people)
1801	240 people
1811	248
1821	289
1831	300
1841	280
1851	331
1861	385
1871	437
1881	416

1891	465
1901	397
1911	489
1921	519
1931	1240
1951	4966
1961	14528

There are no accurate figures for Cranham's population between the 11th and 18th centuries, but for the period of 700 years the population did not vary much from around the 200 figure, even then the next hundred years saw an increase only to 397. During the next ten years the population increased a further hundred, when there was a move to develop the area between Front and Moor Lanes by selling off building plots. In 1907 there was a sale of 65 freehold plots, which, had they all been sold, would have increased the population by about 250, but it seems from the figures that the scheme did not go well, as one of the chief difficulties was supplying water to this part of Cranham. Following this any building that did take place was along the main arteries of St Mary's Lane, Front Lane and Moor Lane. Purely by this type of ribbon development, the population again doubled between 1921 and 1931, but it was not until the break-up of the manors that building on a large scale started. In Cranham's case the sale of the Cranham manor estate (the Benyon Estate) took place in 1937 and much of the farmland was sold off in lots. Lot 8, for example, was the area between Moor Lane and the railway line, where all the roads with bird names are now. South of the railway to St Mary's Lane the 35 acre lot was laid out for housing with the roads taking names of the Bishoprics of England. South of St Mary's Lane, the triangular plot bounded by Pike Lane on one side and the Grays railway line on the other was developed by F G Legg, who started building on this 100 acre site just before the 1939 War. On the outbreak of hostilities only the roads of

Westbury Terrace and Ashvale Gardens had been built, and with the cessation of building during the War and the Green Belt Act post-war, the completion of this ambitious scheme was thwarted, although sewage pipes had already been laid across the fields to Pike Lane in anticipation of the completion of the project. The War also put a stop to the building of a railway station at Cranham on the Grays line by Wantz Bridge, where Judith Anne Court is today. Cranham's population explosion was between 1951 and 1961 when numbers tripled with the development of the land between Front Lane and Moor Lane and also the Avon Road estate.

Cranham Church before 1873

TITHES & HERALDRY

In compiling this short history of Upminster and Cranham I came across information that did not neatly fit into the preceeding chapters, so I have placed these assorted items in this section, hoping that it will be interesting, but at the same time I apologise if the subjects are disparate.

TITHES

In Chapter 4 the problems that the Rector had in collecting tithes from his parishioners were detailed. The incumbent had the right to claim one tenth of all that was produced in the parish to help with the upkeep, and to carry on the work, of the church. Over the years there had always been disputes between residents and the church over the inequalities of the tithe system and it must be appreciated that these disputes were not just local to Upminster, but a problem that plagued the whole country. As time went by many parishioners made private agreements with the Rector for an annual cash payment in lieu of part of the crop or animals. With inflation, naturally these fixed sums depreciated in value and often Rectors gave notice that they wished to revert to tithes in kind.

As early as 1588 there is record of William Latham being in dispute over tithes with the incumbent, William Washer: the matter was settled by arbitration. The difficulties really started when the second member of the Holden family took over the living and in John Rose Holden's first year, 1799, he quarrelled with many of his parishioners over the question of tithes. The dispute and its solution is related in Chapter 4.

Mr Branfil of Upminster Hall was put forward by some of his Essex landowning friends for appointment as one of the Chief Commissioners under the Tithe Commutation Act to be an independent surveyor. As it happens he was unsuccessful, but, as far as the church is concerned, it was probably a good thing, for he would probably have used his influence to obtain a lower tithe assessment for the parish to the detriment of the Rector's income. Although feeling was running high at the time of the 1837 Act, it was not until 1842 that Upminster was surveyed and assessed at an annual figure of £1,052 to be paid by all the landowners to the Rector according to the acreage they owned.

This document and its accompanying map are lodged in the Essex Record Office in Chelmsford (reference D/CT 373 A & B). From it a picture of Upminster in the mid-19th century can be built up. The total acreage was 3,373, made up - Arable, 1,942 acres; Meadow or pasture, 1,011; Houses and roads, 179; Common land, 149; Woodland, 92. The total includes 23 acres of Glebe Land.

As can be seen the majority of Upminster was farmland of one sort or another with only 5% as houses and roads. The survey document then goes on to list all the landowners and their acreages. In all there were only 65 landowners in Upminster in 1842, although some only owned land, with no property on it.

	Acres	Rods	Perches	Rent charge £
Agar, Thomas	141	-	1	58.8.6
Alexander, Henry	30	2	3	10.16.0
Alexander, Thomas		1	16	-
Barber, Susan	5	3	9	0.5.9
Balliscombe, Rev.	23	2	13	8.4.0
Banks, Thomas		1	56	0.0.9
Beardlock, John			14	-
Beardlock, Walter			10	-
Beardlock, Peter			21	-
Brackwell, Captain	31	3	-	11.5.6
Branfil, Champion Edward	672	2	-	228.14.2
Trustees of Champion R Branfil	259	1	-	87.15.5
Brett, John		2	7	0.5.0
Cloth Workers' Company	46	1	29	14.5.6
Clayton, Rev. John	118	1	-	55.8.0
Clayton, George	64	1	-	19.18.0
Colls, William	130	1	-	63.5.6
Cox, Philip Zachariah	80	1	-	28.6.9
Crofs, John	23	3	-	7.15.3
Curtis, Thomas	2	-	-	0.9.6

Name				
Danford, John	1	-	-	-
Dear, Thomas		1	18	-
Eastern Counties Railway	11	2	22	2.13.0
Eldred, John		1	18	-
Esdaile, James		1	23	0.2.6
Felt Makers' Company	40	2	14	15.8.6
Holden, Rev. John Rose	150	2	27	48.12.0
Haws, James	33	3	1	9.7.0
Hawkins, Joseph		2	1	-
Helm, Thomas	86	-	29	28.2.0
Hammond, Samuel	2	1	-	0.8.6
Hammond, William	1	3	-	0.7.6
Harmer, James	65	2	-	25.16.3
Harris, Thomas			7	-
Higgins, James		1	8	-
Jegge, William	23	3	28	7.17.0
Joslin, Henry		1	37	-
King, John		1	2	-
Lee, Joseph		2	-	-
Lennard, Sir Thomas Barrett	180	2	-	52.10.9
Lennard, Thomas Barrett	5	3	29	2.6.9
Manning, William	10	2	-	3.12.3
Marbin, William			39	-
Marshall, Thomas	56	-	12	19.15.6
Mashiter, Thomas	37	3	18	12.5.0
Mears, Benjamin			21	-
Meekins, Isaac			23	-
Mumford, John	15	1	-	5.7.3
New College, Oxford	10	3	24	1.11.0
Nokes, Thomas	48	1	-	16.8.0
Nokes, William	59	2	15	21.14.3
Trustees of Rev. C Ord	249	1	-	53.18.6
Penny, Rev. William	21	1	13	7.0.0
Executors of James Pinchon	1	2	29	1.7.6
Price, Thomas	54	-	36	23.7.0
Purvis, Rev. Richard	158	2	-	43.11.6
Reynolds, Richard	15	2	-	4.19.0
Roper, William	95	2	19	26.0.0
Rowe, George		2	7	-
Rudd, Lydia		3	-	0.4.0
Sterry, Wasey	11	1	2	4.5.3
Towers, Christopher Thomas	4	3	24	1.14.0
Tabrum, Dr. William	4	3	31	1.14.6

Wood, Elizabeth	38	3	12	14.10.0
Holden, Rev. J R (Church & Glebe) 23	-	-	-
Commons	148	1	15	-
Roads & waste	63	1	33	-

	3373	2	33	1052.0.0

From this list the largest landowners can be picked out: their lands were –

Branfil family   932 acres   Upminster   Hall   Manor.
Both sides of Hall Lane. The 259 acres owned by the Trustees were in
the south of the parish in the Sunnings Lane and Aveley Road area.
Trustees of Rev. C Ord   249 acres   Tylers Hall Farm (Upmin-
ster Common) and other land off Tomkyns Lane.
Lennard family   185 acres   Owners of Belhus Estate,
Aveley, part of which was in the parish of Upminster.
Clayton family   182 acres   Gaynes   Manor   estate.
Hoppy Hall farm, together with all the land on the west of Corbets
Tey Road.
Rev. Richard Purvis   158 acres   Great Tomkyns farm
Rev. J R Holden   150 acres   Pages   farm
Thomas Agar   141 acres   Park   Corner   farm
William Colls   130 acres   Hunts farm
Nokes family   107 acres   Land on both sides of
Upminster Hill, the Windmill and also Tadlows, Corbets Tey Road.
William Roper   95 acres   House & farm west of
Nag's Head Lane.
Thomas Helm   86 acres   Great House, Hall Lane
Philip Zachariah Cox   80 acres   Harwood Hall estate.
James Harmer   65 acres   New Place mansion
Thomas Marshall   56 acres   Bramble   farm
Thomas Price   54 acres   Londons

One of the more interesting observations is the relationship
between the Upminster Hall estate of the Branfils and the
Gaynes manor in the ownership of the Clayton family. In
1086 Upminster Hall, then owned by Waltham Abbey, had
about 1,490 acres, while Gaynes was about 1,580. It is
amazing that over nearly 800 years Upminster Hall estate
only fell from 1,490 to 932 acres; meanwhile Gaynes diminished from 1,580 to only 182 acres. As has been seen,
however, following the Claytons, the Joslins once again
built up the estate by buying back Hunts, Hoppy Hall and
Londons, so that by the time the estate was finally broken

up in 1928 the total acreage had crept up to 404.

The second largest landowner was the late Rev. Ord, owning 249 acres in the northeast of the parish. It is significant that the Rector of St Laurence owned 150 acres in his own right: when one sees, in addition, the names of the Rev. Purvis and the Rev. Clayton as large landowners, it is clear that the clergy of those days were wealthy people.

As well as recording the owners of the land and its acreage, the 1842 survey of Upminster also recorded the names of some of the tenants. Although it has not been possible to ascertain all the residents' names, it has been possible to reconstruct where all the houses, cottages and farms were located. The Census of 1841 recorded Upminster's population as 1,117, with 215 properties in the parish. By plotting all the properties mentioned in the survey on a map the result is quite interesting. They all seem to fall neatly into four areas within the parish. Besides the obvious areas of the central crossroads at the 'Bell' corner and Corbets Tey, there was also a small community in Hacton and a much larger grouping around the north of the parish encompassing Nag's Head Lane, Shepherds Hill, Hall Lane north and Tomkyns Lane. Assuming an average of 5 persons to each family (in the mid-19th century the average number of children was 3) the approximate population of the four areas works out –

Village centre	474
Corbets Tey	306
Upminster North	254
Hacton	83

It is revealing how spread the population was and it is of interest that in the area north of the A127 there were about 50 properties – more than there are today. Corbets Tey had its major concentration of houses around the 'Huntsman and Hounds' public house, called the 'Fox and Hounds' in 1842; there were, though, many cottages between Corbets Tey village centre and the south of the parish in the Sunnings/Bramble Lanes vicinity and on the road to Aveley – all of which are included in the Corbets Tey figures.

The survey also gives an insight into the occupation of some of the inhabitants by the description of their dwellings. In 1842 Corbets Tey could boast two public houses, the 'Fox and Hounds' and 'The George', while

Upminster only had the 'Bell' Inn. All three principal districts had a blacksmith and there was a windmill on Upminster Common, as well as the one on Upminster Hill. Corbets Tey was fortunate in having a bakehouse, butchers, slaughterhouse, wheelwright and shoemaker. Upminster only seems to have had a butchers, bakers and a carpenter.

There is also reference in the survey to the Eastern Counties Railway owning 11 acres of land: this was not the Southend line passing through Upminster centre, as this was not built till much later, but refers to the Shoreditch-- Chelmsford line running along the extreme northern edge of the parish for about a mile in the Harold Wood area.

The survey document and its map are well worth consulting, as this is the only detailed plan of the parish since the Domesday survey of 1086. It shows that less than 150 years ago Upminster was still a farming community, wholly reliant on the land for its income, with few shops and businesses in the area. Owner occupation in 1842 was only 30%, compared with 50/60% today.

HERALDRY

Before tracing Upminster's heraldic associations the origins and development of heraldry should be explained. The first signs began to develop at the time of the Norman Conquest: Harold's army at Hastings can be imagined, all in various groups with their lords and knights all dressed in chain mail, with a close fitting steel cap. With everyone looking much the same, both friend and foe, it was possible that foot soldiers in battle would follow the wrong leader with resultant confusion. Recognition was achieved by the leaders carrying distinctive marks in bold colours on their shields The shield thus developed as the central theme of identification and everything else in addition to the shield was of lesser importance.

Heraldry emerged more formally about a century later, when the King would send his royal heralds through- out the country making proclamations, including information about forthcoming tournaments. The royal heralds would keep lists of participating knights as they arrived in London, together with particulars of their coats of arms for identification purposes. From this duty of the royal heralds, which also included giving advice to knights wishing to adopt a coat of arms and settling disputes, that heraldry took its name. Finally, in the reign of Richard III in 1484, the College of Arms was incorporated.

When one sees the coat of arms of a noble family, some institution or a local authority, there is always much more to it than just the shield. The whole 'achievement', as it is called, also incorporates the crest – usually depicted as an object on top of a helmet – over the shield. The object is usually an animal, in the 12th and 13th centuries the crests were often plumes of feathers attached to the nobleman's helm. Animals, often mythical, are sometimes depicted on two legs on either side of the shield and these are called 'supporters'. Under the shield is often a motto, which in England is never now included in the grant of arms and, consequently, it is possible for two people to have the same motto or it is allowable for some one to change their motto if they so wish.

It is surprising how many of Upminster's gentry had their own shields or coats of arms and Wilson in *Sketches of Upminster* lists about 30 arms for Upminster residents over the years. Much of Wilson's research was conducted in St Laurence Church, where a number of arms can be seen on the windows, on mural tablets and in the churchyard.

If, on looking round St Laurence or researching in other places, shields are seen that are not identical to those described below, then possibly the shield belongs to another branch of the family or, possibly, the wife has had her shield 'impaled' on her husband's. A woman has the courtesy right to her father's arms and, when she marries a man who is himself armigerous, then the wife's arms are often shown on the right-hand side, the husband's on the left. The 6 shields described relate to the principal owners of the manors of Gaynes and Upminster Hall. The heraldic word for the description of the shield is 'blazon' and an interpretation of the heraldic words is included.

GAYNES MANOR

ENGAYNE (1218-1360s)

Blazon   Gules, a fess dancette or, between six coss croslets or.

Interpretation Background red, a horizontal jagged band of gold, between six gold crosses.

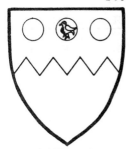

ENGAYNE   DEYNCOURT   LATHAM

DEYNCOURT (1393-1543)

Blazon   Argent, a fess dancette sable, between nine billets sable.

Interpretation Background silver, a horizontal jagged band of black, between nine black bricks.

LATHAM (1543-1641)

Blazon   Or, a chief indentured azure, three roundels argent on the centre on a martlet.

Interpretation Background gold, the top third being blue with a wavy edge, three silver circles with a small bird in the centre circle.

ESDAILE   WALTHAM ABBEY   BRANFILL

ESDAILE (1770-1839)

Blazon   Gules, a lion's head erased or, between three etoiles or.

Interpretation Background red, a lion's head with a jagged edge at its neck in gold, between three six-pointed stars with waved edges.

UPMINSTER HALL

WALTHAM ABBEY (1000–1540)
Blazon   Argent, on a cross engrailed sable five crosses croslet fitchee or.

Interpretation Background silver, with a black cross with semi-circular indentations along the sides on which are five gold crosses with a pointed lower end.

BRANFIL (1685–1920)
Blazon   Or, on a bend gules three mullets argent.

Interpretation Background gold, with a red diagonal band (top left hand to bottom right hand corners) on which are three pointed stars in silver.

A visit to the stained glass window in the north wall of St Laurence Church will show a number of the shields described. The mural tablets round the church contain other shields and, in the churchyard, are the arms of the Rowe and Knapton families.

Upminster Hall Lodge

Photo. by McNamara & Sons, Romford

Upminster Hall Lodge

SOURCES OF REFERENCE

T L Wilson, Sketches of Upminster (1856); T L Wilson, The history and topography of Upminster (1880-1); Scrapbooks of T L Wilson [housed in Essex Record Office]; Upminster Local History Group, The story of Upminster (1957-62, 14 volumes); Anthony D Butler, Upminster Mill (1968); Anthony D Butler, Thirteen centuries of witness (1984); V Body, The Upminster story; E G Ballard, Our old Upminster and district; E G Ballard, Our old Romford and district; A little guide to the Parish Church of St Laurence, Upminster (1965); A short history of Cranham and its Parish Church (1966); Charles K Aked, William Derham and the Artificial Clockmaker (1970); Harold Priestley, John Stranger (1960); Harold Priestley, Essex crime and criminals (1986); Victoria County History, Essex; P Morant, The history and antiquities of Essex (1768); Havering History Review, the journal of the Hornchurch & District Historical Society.